# WHAT'S
## YOUR
# AND?

How sharing your personal passions improves work performance, builds culture, and strengthens relationships with colleagues and clients (and bosses, too)

**Unlock the Person
Within the Professional**

# WHAT'S
# YOUR
# AND?

**John Garrett**

Foreword by **LOU HOLTZ**

**PAGE TWO** BOOKS

Cataloguing in publication information is available from
Library and Archives Canada.
ISBN 978-1-989603-80-2 (paperback)
ISBN 978-1-989603-81-9 (ebook)

Page Two
www.pagetwo.com

Edited by Chris Murray
Copyedited by Crissy Calhoun
Proofread by Alison Strobel
Cover design by Peter Cocking
Interior design by Setareh Ashrafologhalai
Interior illustrations by Stacie Stewart

WhatsYourAnd.com

*To Brooke and my family*

# Foreword

## by Lou Holtz

John Garrett and I first met when we were both at the University of Notre Dame. I was the head football coach and he was a trombone player in the marching band. We met again recently when we were both speaking at a conference in New Orleans.

I was encouraged to hear that we share a core belief and a rule in life: "Show people you care." It's such a simple thing to show you care about those around you. Over time, it builds trust, and I believe that in order to be successful, in life and in your career, people have to trust you.

In this book, John explores why this rule is often set aside when we get to the office. People focus on finishing their assigned tasks instead of focusing on others. Yet, from my experience, you need to recognize that every person you come in contact with at work is asking this question: "Do you care about me?" Don't leave this question unanswered. John explains how to make it very obvious to your coworkers that you care about each and every one of them.

As the head football coach at Notre Dame, it was my responsibility to make sure every player knew I truly cared about them. Not only did I care about their play on the field, I cared about them graduating. I cared about their families, their problems, and their successes. This built the trust necessary for us to have such a successful team year in and year out.

Can you say the same for everyone you work with? Your clients? Your coworkers? Your team at work is no different than my football team in the locker room. As John explains in these pages, if you care about others at work and find out about their outside-of-work passions, you'll create a winning team that everyone wants to be a part of. It's crucial that you show people you care. John has embraced this, and I'm excited for you to read his book to learn how small adjustments make a world of difference. *What's Your "And"?* will inspire and encourage you to show people you care as a matter of practice.

**LOU HOLTZ** FORMER HEAD COACH, NOTRE DAME FOOTBALL
AUTHOR OF *WINNING EVERY DAY, THREE RULES FOR LIVING A GOOD LIFE,* AND FOUR OTHER BOOKS

# Preface

## What Did You Do Last Weekend?

On a cool Monday morning in April, I sat in my cubicle, staring at my computer screen. I was a senior financial analyst so I had month-end work to do. I was just starting what would be hours of careful statistical analysis, looking at endless columns of figures, as I prepared the financial statements and corresponding statistics for my company.

Twelve hours earlier, I had been flying home from Atlantic City where I'd spent the weekend doing four sold-out comedy shows at the Borgata's 1,000-seat Music Box theater, opening for Louie Anderson. I learned a lot from one of the best comedians of all time about the craft of stand-up comedy—connecting with each person in the audience, understanding that the nonverbal performance is just as much a part of the joke, working during the day to make tweaks to the material to try that night, and so much more.

Now that I was back sitting in my cubicle, I realized I was the same person I had been before my Atlantic City trip, yet the difference in how I felt was palpable. Coming into the office that morning, no one announced, "He has a comedy album on satellite radio and you've heard him on *The Bob & Tom Show*. Please welcome to the stage... John Garrett!" My coworkers weren't judging every single move and word I said, deciding whether or not to laugh. And thank goodness there weren't any hecklers! What I wished most, though, was that when I finished my work for the day, I'd say, "Have a good night!" and the rest of the department would applaud as I walked out.

I was still fairly new to comedy, having only been doing it for a few years, and Louie was very gracious to give me the opportunity. I'm sure if anyone in the audience knew I was a CPA, they would've viewed me in a different light. They'd probably even say things like, "You're pretty funny... for an accountant." Yet no one would ever think to say, "You're really good at Excel... for a comedian."

Because the thing is that I was both an accountant *and* a comedian. It was impossible to separate one from the other. I had passed the CPA exam and had all the skills necessary to do that job really well. And I had also worked hard, getting on stage as often as I could, to hone my craft as a comedian.

The added bonus I found is that the skills from one discipline often enhanced the skills of the other. Who doesn't appreciate someone with a sense of humor, especially if they're your internal auditor? How was I supposed to leave a part of me behind when I went to work?

# Author's Note

## I Didn't Get Here Alone

Have you ever believed something to the point that you had to prove it to yourself? Especially if it was something that could improve the lives of so many people? In September 2015, I set out on the journey that led to this book. Without completely knowing what I was doing, I launched *The Green Apple Podcast* (later renamed *What's Your "And"?*). Over the last five years, I have interviewed hundreds of professionals from all over the world who have brought their hobbies and outside-of-work interests to the workplace. As I heard each person talk about how their passions had impacted their career, my own curiosity turned to conviction. My experiment to test this theory has now grown into a movement to change workplace cultures for the better. I knew that together we could shatter the myth of the stereotypical professional.

Throughout this book, you will get glimpses into the lives of these professionals, taken from my podcast interviews, that offer lessons in sharing your "And." I am grateful to my podcast guests for their time and their wisdom. Some are executives who encourage their employees to talk about their hobbies and passions. Most importantly, all are successful professionals who lead the way by sharing their "And" in their workplaces.

Find more information on each of these outstanding individuals in the Meet the Guests section near the end of this book. Or feel free to listen to their entire interviews, and the interviews of hundreds of others, wherever you listen to podcasts.

In the spirit of this book, I have identified these guests by their "And."

# WHAT'S YOUR "AND"?

ook, I get it ...

L You don't have a lot of time because you're busy working and you're exhausted. I'm also going to assume that whatever you do, you are good at your job.

I know because I used to be the exact same way. The last thing you have time for is reading a long business book. And, trust me, the last thing I have time for is writing a long business book. That's why I'll keep this to the essentials: You're so much more than your job title. You're a professional *and* something else.

You may also be an artist.

A cyclist.

A baker.

A volunteer.

A musician.

And the list goes on.

It's time that we all start to recognize this. Because ignoring your "And" makes you less successful and less professional—and it also makes your *organization* less successful.

So, you need to read this book. Your boss needs to read this book. Your direct reports need to read this book. Especially if they have a couple of college degrees and letters after their name.

At the same time, I realize this book isn't for everyone. If you're too timid to make a change or don't have the courage to believe that your vulnerabilities are actually your strengths, then this book isn't for you. If you feel that all activities in an office should have project codes, then this book isn't for you. And if you believe that your identity solely stems from your work, then this book *definitely* isn't for you.

But if you are open to being vulnerable and open to truly getting to know those you work with, then I'm excited to welcome you to the future of professionalism!

# A Limited View of Professionalism

I started performing stand-up comedy after realizing I needed a creative challenge to help balance out my job at PwC. The first time I went on stage, my goal was to not be the absolute worst person who had ever tried to perform comedy. I never dreamed of later having the opportunity to meet comedy legends like Jay Leno, Jerry Seinfeld, Jimmy Brogan, Wayne Cotter, and Louie Anderson. Early on, I was okay at it, but I certainly wasn't on a fast track to *The Tonight Show*.

At the same time, I was promoted to senior associate and hand-selected to be on the team that served the largest financial services client PwC had. I then worked for several companies in the health care industry, doing product contracts, leading business development efforts, and, in my last position, consolidating the financial statements for a large hospital network.

Sure, I took vacation time to perform shows with Louie in Atlantic City or a corporate event with Wayne Cotter in Florida. I also periodically had a comedy club show out of town: I'd leave work at five o'clock to drive to Louisville—or Dayton, or Fort Wayne, or South Bend, or Cincinnati—only to return home that night and be back in the office the next morning.

My passion for stand-up comedy didn't interfere with my work. Ever.

Yet one manager in another department felt that having an outside-of-work interest was "unprofessional," going so far as to say to me in a meeting, "Why don't you just go do your comedy thing? That's all you want to do anyway."

This manager believed in a limited and shallow definition of professionalism: If your whole life is consumed by your career, you're professional; if you have other interests, you're unprofessional. And don't even think about talking about those interests with coworkers.

# A Limited View of Professionalism, Part 2

Unfortunately, that manager is not alone in the way he viewed professionalism.

Andrew Logan, a senior partner at Canadian accounting firm Teed Saunders Doyle & Co., described a similar experience at one of the large international firms early in his career in the 1980s.

At the time, he happened to like having long hair. Clearly his longer hair didn't affect his ability to be a good accountant; he had passed the CPA exam and had worked his way up to manager.

One day, a new managing partner transferred to his office. This new managing partner decided to have one-on-one meetings to get to know each of the managers. While he was at lunch with Andrew, the partner said, "May I offer you some advice?"

Anticipating some encouraging nugget of wisdom, Andrew replied, "Absolutely!"

He said, "Get your hair cut."

I thought, "You know what? No, I don't think I will. I like my hair the way it is. It's kind of who I am." But I think about that conversation a lot. It wasn't about me cutting my hair or not; it's about letting somebody be who they are and not conform to some stereotypical, army-like cutout, if you will. I think that was a defining moment for me, for sure. I've carried that through with my firm here, and as I've progressed up the food chain, I think about that. If somebody wants to wear their hair long or they want to grow a mustache or a beard, it's all good.

**ANDREW LOGAN** HARLEY-DAVIDSON RIDER

And it's also "all good" if someone has outside-of-work hobbies or passions. The only behaviors that should be considered unprofessional are those that make it difficult for you or those around you to do their jobs. Anything and everything up to that point should be completely fine.

# What Is Professionalism?

Let's check *Merriam-Webster.*

professionalism

*noun*

pro·fes·sion·al·ism | \prə-ˈfesh-nə-ˌli-zəm, -ˈfe-shə-nə-ˌli-\
1: the conduct, aims, or qualities that characterize or mark
a profession or a professional person

First of all, I don't know where you went to elementary school, but I was never allowed to define a word by using the same word—and the dictionary did it twice! Not only that, but this is a rather vague definition.

If you really think about it, "the conduct, aims, or qualities" that characterize a professional person have changed over time. In the 1930s, employees at the National Westminster Bank were required to live in smaller houses than their immediate supervisors. At the time, that was considered professional. Until the mid-1940s, employees at the Commercial Bank of Scotland were required to get their boss's permission to marry someone. At the time, that was considered professional. Then by some point in the 1980s, we stopped referring to people as Mr., Mrs., or Miss and started calling them by their first names. In the 1990s and 2000s, men stopped wearing neckties at the office and women weren't always wearing heels. Over time, we started accepting a more casual dress code at the office.

And today, we don't even need to go to the office at all.

Are the people who were required to ask permission to marry more professional—or better at their jobs—than the ones who now work from home? No, of course not. I would argue that today's professional is much better poised to take on the challenges that come their way.

The "conduct, aims, and qualities" that characterized a professional at various points in history are completely ridiculous by today's standards. We all know times have changed, but our concept of professionalism hasn't fully evolved with it.

It's easier to define "unprofessional": Everything is considered professional until you cross the line of inhibiting someone else's ability to do their job. If you are, then stop doing whatever that is because you're being unprofessional. Otherwise, do whatever you want, provided you still get your work done.

It's that simple.

For so many people in our industry [professional services] when you ask them what they did or what they do, the response will always somehow revolve around work or the need to work or the need to work more than they did. It's because these people still carry the mindset that should be almost dead within our industry but somehow isn't. They believe that the only measure of who they are as an employee is how long they're willing to sit in a chair.

I can remember being a manager and being in an evaluation meeting for senior associates and we're going through this one guy and he had this truly ridiculous, unhealthy amount of charge hours and—I'll never forget—one of the partners said, "That's really impressive." I thought to myself, "Impressive?!? If you want to impress me, go and get a girlfriend or pick up a hobby or do something other than sit here all day." But they were talking about the kid like he was ready to skyrocket to the top because he's willing to sit there the longest. If you think about efficiency, the question is: What kind of value did we get out of those 3,000 hours or whatever it was?

**TONY NITTI** MOUNTAIN BIKER/BACKCOUNTRY SKIER

# Needed Now
# More Than Ever

Computers and automation and AI are changing the way we work. But the one thing that will never change, and is possibly now more obvious than ever, is that business is a human-to-human transaction. Sure, a computer can run lengthy calculations in the fraction of a second or be used for legal research. But can it explain the options to a client who might need a little sympathy?

Unfortunately, we work in a time when we are quickly forgetting our human side. Sure, we have college degrees and certifications, but we also have hobbies and passions and interests outside of work. And these activities are what separate us from AI. Think about it, how many machines have hobbies?

> Find something of yourself to share with colleagues, with journalists, with clients—something that helps you stand out from the rest of the crowd as being a bit different. Don't try and manufacture it. But if you have a particular interest or a hobby, reveal it and share it because A, you'll find other people who may share the same interest and B, it will help them to remember you compared to all of the other people they know who do the same work as you. This approach has proven invaluable to me because, over the years, fellow professionals and journalists have

remembered me. Just recently, I was at an accounting conference where the deputy managing partner of a firm I left twenty years ago remembered me partly because he recalled me doing magic tricks over dinner and at partner's meetings.

**MARK LEE** MAGICIAN

At a time when working remotely is becoming more prevalent, we need to be more intentional to create these human connections. Our only connection to work is a laptop screen. It'd be just as easy for you or anyone on your team to work for another company staring at the same computer screen.

A 2018 ManpowerGroup study found that 45 percent of organizations worldwide cannot fill all their open positions, so talent is at a premium. Adopting the philosophy outlined in this book will help you create a better culture at your organization, which will attract and retain top talent, as well as more ideal clients.

As artificial intelligence completes many of the tasks that once took many hours, it's the *human* side to our professional skills, such as our ability to create empathy and trust with our clients, that are becoming ever more vital to our success in the workplace. Sharing our hobbies and passions brings out our human side to complement our skills, and, as you'll discover in this book, it also makes us happier employees.

# Bring All of Yourself to Work

I've often found that professionals have a hard time truly being themselves when they're in a work setting. They often model the behavior of someone who went before them, who no doubt modeled the behavior of someone who went before them and so on. To the point where no one is actually bringing their true self to work.

This is an issue that has been discussed for centuries, going back to the time of Aristotle. He wrote a lot about the concept of eudaimonia. "Eu" meaning "good" and "daimon" meaning "soul" or "self," the word means "good soul" or "good self." Aristotle believed eudaimonia was the optimal state of human existence. It's not happiness because happiness is fleeting. One moment, you're happy and the next moment, you're not. That yo-yo tendency isn't ideal for organizations; workplace happiness can become workplace frustration in a matter of minutes.

Eudaimonia—the optimal state of human existence— entails bringing all of who you are to all of what you do.

When you're at work, you're the same person.

When you're at home, you're the same person.

When you're with your friends, you're the same person.

When you're engaged in your hobby or passion, you're the same person.

The skills and talents that you develop in one of these areas are forever in your tool belt, and you carry them to all the other areas of your life—even the workplace, whether professionalism likes it or not.

MODULE

1

# ELEVATE THE EMPLOYEE EXPERIENCE

## PART 1

# Sharing Interests Makes Employees More Engaged

# Increasing Engagement

**Organizations with engaged employees
are more productive and profitable.**

Before I talk about how employees who share their "And"
increase their engagement, let me show why engagement is important to the employee and the company.

The numbers are in and they don't lie. An HR.com
research study showed that 90 percent of respondents
believed there was solid evidence linking engagement
to performance, and that engagement had the strongest impact on customer service and productivity. The
survey asked, "In your organization, to what degree
do higher rates of engagement have a positive impact
on the following areas?" Here's how the respondents
answered:

| | | |
|---|---|---|
| Customer service | 41% Very high | 41% High |
| Productivity | 31% Very high | 50% High |
| Product quality | 32% Very high | 43% High |
| Company brand | 34% Very high | 39% High |
| Financial performance | 21% Very high | 42% High |

And here are some more figures I found interesting: 70 percent of all working professionals in a 2018

LinkedIn Workplace Culture survey agreed that they would reject a job at a top company if the employer was known for having a bad workplace culture.

When it comes to looking for a new job, most young adults say a better quality of life at work is more important than a fatter salary, according to a 2016 survey by Fidelity. In fact, twenty-five- to thirty-five-year-olds said they'd be willing to give up an average of $7,600 in pay for a better situation at the office, such as more career development and a healthier work-life balance.

# Not Engaged to the Job, Engaged to the People

## People are more engaged because they are closer to the people they work with.

Based on my experience, I believe that you aren't engaged to your job: you're engaged to the people you work with. Humans crave connection and are built for community. The stronger those human connections are, the more engaged you will be—no matter what your tasks are.

The first step to increasing engagement doesn't require a lot of money or creative ideas. It only requires management to foster an environment where people are encouraged to share their outside-of-work interests. Celebrating these hobbies and shining a light on these passions will draw people closer to each other.

I realized this when I spoke at a partner retreat for a large regional accounting and advisory firm. Three of their partners were retiring, so time was set aside for others to talk about them. There wasn't a single mention of the number of clients they brought in or how much revenue they had made for the firm. Each story was something personal that had occurred outside of work.

The more sharing that occurs, the greater the odds that people start to genuinely care about each other, even if they don't share the same interests.

But it's an even bigger bonus if they do share the same interests because then they have more to talk about besides work. They might also find the time to do that hobby together outside of work, developing stronger bonds that will keep them engaged.

> All of these things that we do outside of work are part of what makes us better when we're at work. It's really exciting because the more we're willing to explore and enjoy our lives and sort of learn new things that aren't part of our official training, I think that makes us better at thinking, better at communicating, better at interacting, better at connecting with coworkers—which ultimately makes us care about each other more.
>
> **RUMBI BWERINOFA-PETROZZELLO** FILM FESTIVAL VOLUNTEER

The people who you talk to about your outside-of-work passions have a different relationship with you. They see you in a different light and are more interested in those other parts of your life. And vice versa. You have a stronger relationship with these folks and are more engaged when you're with them.

If you had your dream job at your dream company but were surrounded by people you couldn't tolerate, you'd quit. On the flip side, I was talking to someone at a professional services firm that had been recently acquired by a larger regional firm. The transition hadn't been very smooth and many people chose to leave. Someone told him, "The reason people are still working here is because of the other people who are still working here."

# Retaining Talent

**People are more likely to stay because they see that others are interested in them.**

People who feel valued and cared for are going to stay with an organization longer. It's that simple. By taking a genuine interest in their passions and interests, you're showing that you are interested in them as people, not just as accountants, lawyers, consultants, or engineers.

> I like having that family-friendly environment—I say "family friendly" but it's more just flexibility to make some lifestyle choices and making sure that each individual is set up for success. This way your employees want to keep coming back and want to come and do good work.
>
> **BROOKE MORTENSEN** FRENCH HORN PLAYER

A large client of mine had been through a lot of changes in the years after filing for bankruptcy. They had massive turnover in every department—except IT. This team of fifteen people had been together for many years. I was very curious why, and was excited to have the opportunity to speak at the department's off-site retreat. I decided to have each person introduce themselves to me and then asked the rest of the group to tell me what that person's outside-of-work hobby or passion was. For every single person in the group, at least four of the others knew the answer. I was amazed and told them, "And that's why you've had zero turnover. You genuinely care about each other."

That being said, the goal is not for an entire company to have zero percent turnover. There will always be people who move for a variety of reasons; maybe they want to relocate to a different city, for example, or need more room for advancement. Some are okay to lose but many are not.

We just don't ever want the reason to be that they didn't feel the people around them were sincerely interested in them. We don't want them leaving because their colleagues—including you—didn't take the time to learn what they're truly passionate about.

# The Cost
# of Turnover

### Employees who feel connected to
### other employees are more likely to stay.

Lower turnover is a huge boost to the financial success of your firm or company. Recent studies have shown that it costs your organization 1.5 to 2 times that person's annual salary to recruit, interview, hire, and train a new individual to fill a role. This includes the lost productivity as the new person gets up to the output speed of the person who left. Multiply that by each person who leaves and it's easy to see this is a significant amount of money. Turnover should not be taken lightly. For instance, an office of 100 people with an average salary of $100,000 and 15 percent turnover costs an organization over $2 million. Every. Single. Year.

Reducing turnover is also the best way to foster talent who can develop into the future leaders of your organization. While you can certainly hire from outside, why take that risk when you can mold them from within? That way, you know for sure that the person you promote already fits your culture and follows the same procedures.

Leadership transition will be smoother as well since the person has spent years building connections. They have relationships with both clients and coworkers, which took time to develop, and those connections allow for a seamless transition.

> The folks who have those outside commitments that they pursue year over year with seriousness—that is a marker of someone who is a committed professional. It's a marker of somebody who's going to be successful and engaged... I want to know what's going on in their lives because that's going to make me a better leader. It's going to make me a better team member. And it's going to to make the folks we work with more invested in what we're all driving toward.
>
> **ALI METZL**  MARATHONER

# Your Passions Deepen
# Your Relationships

**Your outside-of-work interests aren't
distractions. They're relationship enhancers.**

You're not the only one who has interests outside of
work. You know who else does? Clients. Coworkers. The
people you're around for forty-plus waking hours each
week. The people you rely on to make work happen. Better relationships with all of them is always a good thing.

> There are a lot of us that run and train together. It's certainly a conversation piece with everyone—both with coworkers and clients. I think that there's a bonding experience when we train together and it's something that lets us relate to each other. It's been very touching how many clients and business associates follow when my next race is. That's one of the first things they say to me: "How is the training going?" or "When's the next one?" The local news has even interviewed me, and clients—even prospective clients—have called me and said, "Oh, I saw you on TV."
>
> **DONNA BRUCE** MARATHONER

Imagine if you found out that a client worked on
cars, just like you do. Or you found out that a coworker
was also passionate about bird-watching. Or about

science-fiction movies. You're suddenly best friends and have something more to talk about besides work. Your relationship becomes sticky and is different than your relationships with other coworkers.

Maybe you're thinking, "Sure, John, but no one else in my office loves *my* hobby—playing pinball!" First of all, how do you know if you don't share your love of pinball?

I was once on stage at a firm's all-staff meeting and I asked an employee what she loved to do outside of work. She told me, "It's really boring."

I told her, "I'll be the judge of that. What is it?"

Immediately after she said, "Genealogy," a woman across the room blurted out, "That's not boring—I do that, too!"

They had been working four cubicles apart from each other for years and never knew they shared the same passion. The only way this could get any better is if they shared their family trees and discovered they were distant cousins going back to the 1600s.

But even if you don't share the same hobby, great connections can still happen if you're both willing to share. I'd never met anyone in my company who also does comedy, but that didn't stop my coworkers from coming in on Monday morning and asking me about my shows. I've never ridden a motorcycle but that never stopped me from asking one of my coworkers about her road trips.

# Sharing Passions Supercharges Morale

**Employees are more likely to stay because talking about their interests boosts morale.**

Have you ever noticed what happens when you talk to people about their hobbies or passions? Their eyes light up. There's an energy in their voice. They smile. Every time.

Have you ever noticed what happens when someone talks about work? Sometimes they might light up. But definitely not every time.

If you need a morale booster in your office, start talking to people about what they love to do outside of work. When I talked with Hannah Horton and Abby Parsons, two auditors who decided to start taking fiddle lessons together, they talked about how despite being absolute beginners at playing the fiddle, sharing this hobby at work provided everyone something to talk about besides work. It provided an energy for everyone to feed off. And they smiled. People in other departments were recognizing them as "the fiddle players," which made them stand out among the other employees who also had accounting degrees.

The firm is pretty big and we have a lot of different departments. Pretty much, I only know the people in the audit
department. Now people will be like, "Oh, wait. Are you the
one that plays the fiddle?" People that I don't even usually
talk to or even know who they are.

**HANNAH HORTON** FIDDLER

We're around these people more than our families;
why not have all those waking hours be a little more
enjoyable? Sharing stories about your outside-of-work
interests and encouraging others to do so as well brings
some emotion to work that might not otherwise be there.

# Passions Aren't Drama

**Seeking attention is not a morale booster.**

It's important for me to say that sharing your interests outside of work doesn't mean bringing drama to the office. Doing so is the very definition of unprofessional. To understand the difference between sharing a passion and something that's not a passion, ask yourself these questions:

"Is this something that brings me joy?"

"Am I only seeking attention by talking about this?"

"Will sharing this interfere with someone else's ability to do their job?"

There are times when we'll have issues that we need to share with others, but doing so on a regular basis is taxing for everyone involved. Common examples are repeatedly bringing up your relationship troubles or the wild drama happening in your life. These things don't bring you joy, and they are often shared to get attention. When shared excessively, such drama can interfere with other people's ability to do their jobs.

# PART 2

## Sharing Interests Makes Employees More Successful

# Broaden the Definition of "Expertise"

**It's so much more than your technical skills.**

If I asked you about your expertise, you would no doubt start with the skills you've developed earning your college degrees and other certifications. In some way or another, you use these skills to be successful at your job. *Merriam-Webster* defines expertise as "the skill of an expert." Again, what's with the dictionary using the word in the definition of the word?! So, I looked up "expert" and *Merriam-Webster* defines it as "having, involving, or displaying special skill or knowledge derived from training or experience."

But what if we are defining our professional expertise too narrowly? Skills learned from experiences outside of work can make you better at your job. Today's professionals possess skills learned above and beyond their degrees or certifications—skills they learned pursuing their outside-of-work interests.

What if we realized each individual brings a unique skill set to the office? There's a huge untapped well of expertise and talent sitting in your office right now. When you look at expertise more holistically, you begin to see how to use people's skills in a way that is more effective for both the organization and the individual.

For instance, Ben Westbrook is a director of tax operations and he also used to sing opera. When it comes to deciding who will give a presentation in front of an audience, he should be strongly considered. So often, the person chosen is the one who's been at the company longest, and that's rarely the right choice.

When it comes to presenting to a client, would it be best to choose the person who has been on stage singing opera or the person who loves to do jigsaw puzzles? Clearly, the person who is used to performing in front of an audience is much better suited for this. Not only that, performing is what this individual loves to do, so giving them this opportunity will make them happy and much more engaged with their work.

> A skill that I think I really got from singing opera is just the performance aspect of it. [My supervisor's] like, "Oh, Ben, do you want to get up in front of the firm and talk about this topic for thirty minutes?" I'm like, "Yeah, sure. I've got this." I know how to deal with my nerves. I know how to present things. I'm very comfortable doing that. It's a skill that a lot of people in accounting are very uncomfortable with. I think that has helped me a lot. It doesn't bother me to have to get up and do that.
>
> **BEN WESTBROOK** OPERA SINGER

But what if an organization never takes the time to find out about its employees' hobbies or passions? What if a manager selects the jigsaw puzzle person instead of the community theater performer, dancer, or opera singer? Not only is the presentation going to suffer, but this jigsaw puzzle champ is also likely to feel a little uncomfortable. Meanwhile, the employees with stage experience get frustrated that they weren't selected. If you make these kinds of choices enough over time, employees will become disengaged and eventually quit. All because their manager didn't take the time to discover the latent expertise in their department.

# Clients Will
# Trust You More

## People do business with people
## they know, like, and trust.

There's a common phrase in the professional world that
"people do business with people they know, like, and
trust." Notice the phrase isn't "people do business with
people who are the best at what they do." And it isn't
"people do business with people who call themselves
trusted advisors," or "people do business with people
who have been doing it the longest."

The truth of this statement—that people do business
with people they know, like, and trust—was proven in
a study by Daniel Kahneman and Amos Tversky. They
won a Nobel Prize, so I think they know what they're
talking about. The study, rooted in cognitive psychology, found that people trust their instincts and would
prefer to choose an option that is certain rather than a
risky choice that has the potential to be better. In other
words, people would rather do business with someone
they like and trust than someone they don't, even—
and here's the kicker—if that likable person's service is
known to be of lower quality or a higher price. Known
service providers are preferred over unknown service

providers even when the decision-maker knows they're not as good.

Which leads me to believe your technical skills are overrated. It's not that they aren't important, they're just not *as* important as we've been led to believe. A Carnegie Foundation study showed that 85 percent of financial success was due to "human engineering" skills: the ability to connect with another person using one's personality. It also factored in the ability to lead and negotiate and to communicate effectively. Additionally, this study showed that only 15 percent of financial success was found to be due to technical knowledge. Fifteen. Percent. The most surprising part of this study is that it was done over a hundred years ago—in 1918.

So, people skills outperform technical skills. And yet what was your entire education focused on? Technical skills. Your continuing education classes? Technical skills. How are people promoted? How are bonuses determined? More often than not, the answers are technical skills and technical skills.

When I'm talking to either clients or other people in the office, I just look for some type of common ground. I have been fortunate enough that I can have either a military thing to share with them or a music thing or a sports thing, so it makes it easy to try to get that first connection with someone and then take that conversation somewhere else. This has been very useful in my career.

**DAVID BEASLEY**  MUSICIAN/COMPOSER

# Technical Skills
# Don't Make a Leader

### Career success is more about relationships than expertise.

It's interesting that a large technology company like Google has recognized that being a good manager takes much more than technical skills. Here are the first eleven questions of the leadership evaluation survey sent to every "Googler" in the company, asking them to rate these qualities on a scale of one to five.

1. My manager gives me actionable feedback that helps me improve my performance.

2. My manager does not "micromanage" (get involved in details that should be handled at other levels).

3. My manager shows consideration for me as a person.

4. The actions of my manager show that they value the perspective I bring to the team, even if it is different from their own.

5. My manager keeps the team focused on our priority results/deliverables.

6. My manager regularly shares relevant information from their manager and senior leaders.

7. My manager has had a meaningful discussion with me about career development in the past six months.

8. My manager communicates clear goals for our team.

9. My manager has the technical expertise (e.g., coding in Tech, selling in Global Business, accounting in Finance) required to effectively manage me.

10. I would recommend my manager to other Googlers.

11. I am satisfied with my manager's overall performance as a manager.

Notice that only one item addresses technical skills. Only one. I believe this same survey could be used for evaluating team members to emphasize the importance of interpersonal skills.

One would think that every professional's ultimate goal would be being well known, liked, and trusted. Yet all of our education and continuing education is spent learning technical skills, rather than teaching us to be known, liked, or trusted. Someone decided to label these as "soft skills," making it seem as if they aren't essential to doing business. This couldn't be further from the truth.

In my research, I've found that some professionals think that emphasizing these non-technical skills is frowned upon in their workplace. I've had survey respondents say that they "don't get paid to get to know each other" or "There isn't a charge code for socializing." But when you get to the bottom of it, you are in fact paid to get to know each other, because that's how projects get done.

It seems most people work from a permission-based mindset, so what if organizations had a charge code or intentionally set time aside for socializing? I'd like to think this would lead to a lot more knowing, liking, and trusting between all of us, which has been proven to lead to better business.

# Being Human > Being Perfect

## Emphasizing technical skills over everything else sets people up for failure.

There's a side effect to the misguided emphasis on technical skills over these more important human skills.

> We're all human. We all have faults. None of us is perfect all the time. And the harder you try to be perfect, the easier it is to fail—or to feel like you failed—no matter how small the mistake. My wife and I have two daughters and if there's one thing that I can instill in them, it's just to say, "You know what? Just be who you are and try your best. If people aren't satisfied with that, it's not your issue, it's their issue."
>
> **JASON HASTIE** COUNTRY MUSIC SINGER/SONGWRITER

It's impossible for us to be absolutely perfect all the time. We're human. Humans become fatigued. Humans make mistakes. No matter how hard we try, it happens. And no amount of technical skills training will completely fix this. Ever.

We're setting up people to feel like failures by pumping them full of technical skills and more technical skills training, which makes them feel like they should never make a mistake. Not only is that not true, but we're completely ignoring the lessons of 100 years of psychological studies.

So, never feel like you're a failure for not being perfect. Try your best but remember you're human. And so are the people around you. As these studies have shown, being human is even better than being perfect.

# PART 3

## Sharing Interests Makes Employees Happier and Healthier

# Your Passion Is Always with You, No Matter the Job

**Passions are your rock, making you feel more grounded and confident.**

No matter your job title or profession, the hobby or passion you have outside of work will be with you forever. Should you get promoted, your job will certainly change—but your hobby or passion won't. Should you take on a new role, the technical skills you use will certainly change—but your hobby or passion won't. Should you move to a different company, your work environment will change—but your hobby or passion won't.

If you think about it, these outside-of-work interests are one of the few constants we have. Everything else will inevitably change over the course of your career: your office, your skills, the people you report to, the technology used.

It's absolutely crucial that you remember your outside-of-work passions or interests. Often these interests were with you before you started your current job. Even if you developed your hobby recently, these interests will always be there for you, even after you retire.

For instance, I love college football. Bowl season is my favorite time of the year because there are games to watch almost every day for nearly three weeks straight.

I loved college football when I was a student.

I loved college football when I was an associate at PwC.

I loved college football when I was promoted to senior associate at PwC.

I loved college football when I worked in Product Contracts at Schwarz Pharma.

I loved college football when I was the business development director at Vesta Pharmaceuticals.

I loved college football when I was a senior financial analyst at Clarian Health Partners.

And I love college football now.

No matter what company I worked for or what title I had or what job I was doing, college football was (and will always be) a part of me. Sure, some years were more fun for me than others, depending on how my team did, but my passion remained constant. The same goes for you and your outside-of-work passions. In a world that is rapidly changing, your hobby or passion is the one thing that will stay constant.

> My mom did say that I could sing before I could talk. I've kind of done that all my life. Lived in Nashville for a little while, not to pursue my music career, but it certainly was fun to be in that scene and to be on Music Row, and I got to meet some really cool artists and producers. That

was fun, just to kind of be in that space. No matter where we've lived, I've always been in choirs or led choirs, from children's choirs up to adult choirs.

**RACHEL FISCH** SINGER/CHOIR DIRECTOR

Professionalism tells us that our passions should be the first thing we abandon when going to work. Professionalism makes us believe that we should leave these passions outside the office. Professionalism means that sharing what we love to do isn't encouraged in most workplaces because there isn't a charge code for doing so.

But your outside-of-work passion is the one thing that remains with you no matter where you go; it's a true source of identity and confidence in an ever-changing world. It's the eye of the hurricane that remains still while changes swirl around you. It's your anchor to keep you grounded and your source of joy when things get stressful.

# The Joy of
# Being Yourself

## Employees shouldn't go home
## exhausted after playing a "part" all day.

I've found that a lot of professionals act at work as if
they are playing a part in a play. They behave like someone they think they're supposed to be, instead of being
themselves. We tell ourselves things like, "This is how
a law partner is supposed to act" or "This is how a manager should be."

And the bigger the difference between your work
character and your real self, the more difficult it gets.
The irony is that trying to hide your true self and
outside-of-work interests is so exhausting that you
end up not having any energy to actually pursue those
interests after you leave the office.

When I talked with Amy Hancock, an engineer who is
also a photographer and published model, she brought
up how stressful it was to lead two lives. She found herself asking, "Who have I shared my modeling with?" and
"How much have I shared with them?" Keeping a part
of herself a secret was absolutely tiring for her, which
drained her energy for photography and modeling.

It's so exhausting. I think I learned to just relax and accept that role. Why does it matter what other people think? The right people are not going to think anything badly of me. In fact, they're probably going to think it's kind of cool. Then when I did open up, I was just like, "You know what? I'm done. I can't hide this anymore." If someone asks me about it, I'm not going to deny it—which I didn't deny it anyway. It was just that I would never initiate any conversation about it. I think, for me, it was just like a big weight off my shoulders.

**AMY HANCOCK**  MODEL/PHOTOGRAPHER

Instead of wasting energy on hiding your interests, you could use that energy to pursue them.

# Reducing Anxiety and Depression

## Putting all your eggs in the work basket heightens anxiety and depression.

People who view themselves as having many dimensions—what psychologists call "self-complexity"—are less prone to anxiety and depression. A Duke University study by Patricia Linville about self-complexity concluded that "subjects higher in self-complexity were less prone to depression, perceived stress, physical symptoms, and occurrence of the flu and other illnesses following high levels of stressful events."

Imagine two different people. They both work hard and are good at their jobs, but only one of them has other interests in their life—whether they are hobbies or family or faith or any other activity outside of the office. These interests give that person additional sources of identity. Meanwhile, the other person doesn't have any interests beyond work, which means their emotional dependence rests solely on their role in the office. This individual, whose entire self-worth is tied up in their career, is going to have a higher level of anxiety about every outcome—whether it's a client deciding to extend a contract or a manager deciding to give that person a raise or promotion. And if a decision doesn't go their way, that's a 100 percent direct blow to their identity. It's especially difficult when they are new to a position and therefore likely to be a little slower or make mistakes as they learn. Depending on how many sources of self-worth a person has, a mistake can easily escalate from "I'm new at this and still learning" to "I'm not very good at my job" to "I'm not a very good person altogether."

The other person—the one with other dimensions to them, such as hobbies and interests outside of work—has several different sources of happiness and confidence. Therefore, outcomes at work don't carry the same weight. Sure, they're important, but they won't deliver the same high levels of anxiety and potential depression as they could for someone without outside-of-work interests.

[Being a fiddler] has made work—not only work, actually both life and work—more enjoyable because it gives us something to talk about that is not just clients and other issues. Once we started sharing that we were taking these fiddle lessons, it spread like wildfire. It was a fun, positive thing we would talk to people about in the middle of what's usually a miserable busy season. It just seemed,

> not only for us but for other people, like a morale booster, like something they would laugh about and talk about.
>
> **ABBY PARSONS** FIDDLER

Just remember that while your job provides income, it isn't a complete picture of who you are. You are much more complex than your job title. The more dimensions you have and the more you share them with others, the happier—and more productive—you will be.

# Make Better
# Ethical Decisions

## More identity overlap
## encourages moral behavior.

Each of us has different identities depending on the situation we are in. In the office, you're a manager. On the basketball court, you're a competitor. At home, you're a spouse and a parent. For some people, these identities are completely different: a motivating manager, a take-no-prisoners competitor, and a nurturing partner and parent. Many of us behave differently depending on our social role, job title, interpersonal relationship, activity, or goal. For others, these self-aspects are consistent regardless of the situation.

A study done by Maferima Touré-Tillery of Northwestern University and Alysson Light of the University of the Sciences introduces the term "self-overlap": "the extent to which people perceive their various self-aspects as interconnected, such that their thoughts and feelings about themselves are similar across these self-aspects ... Specifically, people high in self-overlap (interconnected self-aspects) are more likely to behave ethically than people low in overlap."

I'm going to assume we all agree that behaving ethically makes you a better professional. Based on this research, it's safe to say that having more self-overlap—merging more of your work identity with your outside-of-work identity—will make you a better professional. Touré-Tillery says, "If I tend to think about myself the same way from one identity to the next, then if I do something that's going to make me feel bad about myself, it's likely that I'll feel bad about myself across all of my identities. Every unethical thing amplifies that sense of being a bad person."

Those with more self-overlap realize that their actions at work also affect how we perceive ourselves as a friend, spouse, or parent. This research shows that merging our identities—not compartmentalizing our different selves—makes us more likely to make moral and ethical decisions. By encouraging everyone to merge their work and personal lives, and to share their outside-of-work interests, organizations are in turn encouraging everyone to become better professionals.

# We Need Human Connection

## Be more satisfied with your life.

We are built for human connection. In Maslow's hierarchy of needs, "love and belonging" comes only after both psychological needs and safety needs have been met, but some psychologists feel social connection plays a bigger role than originally thought. Research shows that we desire a sense of belonging and the confidence that comes from friendship. By sharing your outside-of-work interests and passions, you'll be more satisfied with your life. Not your job. Your life.

In Tom Rath's research for his book *Vital Friends*, 96 percent of people surveyed who had three close friends at work were more satisfied with their lives. Ninety-six percent! The auditor in me wants to round that up to 100 percent and call the other 4 percent an "immaterial difference."

You can't make three close friends unless you're willing to open up and show the real you. The simplest way to do this is by letting others hear about your outside-of-work passions and interests. This is also a simple way to combat stress. Studies have shown that social contact is an excellent stress reliever: your network offers you support while also providing a distraction.

The more we try to separate our work life from the rest of our life, the more difficult it gets to look at coworkers as possible friends. And the more hours we spend working, the more this exacerbates feelings of loneliness, which according to former surgeon general of the United States, Vivek H. Murthy, is a public health crisis.

To combat this, we need to allow space and time at work for creating these human connections. A Gallup study suggests that "to have a thriving day, we need *six hours* of social time. When we get at least six hours of daily social time, it increases our well-being and minimizes stress and worry." To get six hours of daily social time during the week, some of that has to take place at work. Are you allowing yourself to do this? Are you allowing others around you to do the same?

As you can see, even casual conversations about things other than work lead to a happier, more engaged team that will produce higher-quality work, which will in turn foster an organization more inclined to attract and retain talent.

Casual conversations and small talk become more difficult as the prevalence of working remotely rises. More effort is required to create meaningful connections because phone calls and video chats don't yield the same results as in-person gatherings.

# Become a Friend, Not a Colleague

## Colleagues become friends when everyone shows their authentic selves.

By sharing your outside-of-work interests, you're showing a little more of your true self to everyone around you. Your relationship status goes from "colleague" to "friend." That benefits an organization in so many ways because it transforms people who work together into people who also genuinely care about each other.

If someone is completely swamped with work and needs some help after regular business hours, a friend will be more inclined than a colleague to stay and help. This results in making the group more efficient and it reduces anxiety in the person with the heavy workload. Being overwhelmed can lead to giving up, taking longer than usual to complete tasks, or calling in sick more often. A friend cares about their coworker and is willing to help that person over a hump, knowing the other person would do the same for them.

If you want to make a friend, you have to be a friend first, and so if you can share a little bit, then you'll be amazed who will come to you and share back... I think other people see that openness, and they're willing to share more with you. It goes back to being a friend. You learned how to make a friend years ago, and yet so many people can't figure out how to make a friend within the business sense to really create the ability to move forward in their own careers.

**JODY PADAR** REALITY TV FAN

Critical feedback also doesn't seem so critical when it comes from someone who you know cares about you. If the only communication a leader has with an employee is related to work, then work is the only connection they have. When that connection is tense, the employee might become disengaged or possibly quit. But if a leader communicates with their team regularly and about a variety of topics, then the negative impact of critical feedback isn't so strong. It feels more like a friend pulling you aside to say, "Hey, I know you can do better."

If you're a leader in your organization, especially in the C-suite or at the partner level, sharing your interests makes people feel less intimidated by your position. As a result, those around you might feel more comfortable raising issues or asking questions without the fear of putting themselves out there. By being more human through sharing your interests, you show a level of trust that they will very likely reciprocate. Equally important, you go from being the CEO or managing partner to someone with a first name. The staff can say, "Hey, why don't you just go ask Stacey?" instead of "Go ask the CEO." Titles can be intimidating, so you need to be intentionally approachable if you want everyone to feel comfortable seeking your input when they need to.

Being curious about people's outside-of-work interests can have an enormous impact on their level of engagement at work. In one study, one-third of respondents believed their manager cared about their personal lives. Of those respondents, 54 percent were engaged at work. Of the two-thirds who did not believe their manager cared about their personal lives, only 17 percent were engaged. It's sad to think that only a third of us think that our managers care about us beyond the scope of our work. But it's not surprising that those of us who feel our managers don't care about us as people are significantly less engaged.

It's such a simple thing to genuinely care about those around us, but we need to intentionally make the time to do so.

# Breathing
# in Happy

**By allowing you time to pursue your passions, your employer is letting you breathe in happy.**

Mark Winburn is an IT systems and controls auditor who also happens to be an amazing singer. Like a really amazing singer. When I talked with him, he told me, "Singing is me breathing in happy."

"What about IT audits?" I asked him.

He answered, "Not so much!"

Think about that for a moment. Breathing in happy. How powerful is that statement?

> It really gets to my heart. When I've just done a performance—as I was explaining to my parents—for me, singing is breathing in happy. You want to live your life and experience the things that you're interested in, and music and singing is what I like to do. I also like to be quietly sitting in a boat, throwing a fishing line in the water. It can't be all work and no play. Somewhere in the middle is that happy medium where folks find purpose and meaning and fulfillment in life.
>
> **MARK WINBURN** SINGER

Singing is his passion and it allows him to breathe in happy. What is it that allows you to breathe in happy?

What is it that allows those around you to breathe in happy?

Unfortunately, it's too easy for us to forget what allows us to breathe in happy because that activity probably doesn't pay the bills. But if you remind yourself that your passions and interests are one of your main sources of happiness, then you will remember to make them a priority. And if employers realized how much more engaged and committed their people are when they are happy, they would encourage them to pursue their interests.

My ultimate dream is for organizations to track each person's "passion hours" in the same way that accounting and law firms track continuing education hours. If you don't have a minimum number of passion hours, then you aren't as effective in your role.

I see organizations make hiring decisions, especially with new hires out of college, based on the ability of qualified candidates to differentiate themselves by being open about their extracurricular activities. But, all too often, those same companies never give their employees the time to continue with those extracurricular activities. Organizations are slowly suffocating these energetic team members by preventing them from breathing in their happy. While they may not explicitly say it this way, this is exactly what happens when leaders make snide comments about having too much fun at work or shoot disparaging looks at small groups bonding in the break room. This toxic workplace culture is also reinforced when a person who works an insane amount of overtime is celebrated, which completely disregards whether such performance can be sustained over time. It's possible that person works such long hours because they're terribly inefficient.

Don't ignore the activities that allow you to breathe in happy. Find what does it for you and encourage those around you to find theirs. If you're sitting there thinking, "My happy is my job," that's fine, but I'd like to invite you to ignite new interests. It will add to your overall happiness and job performance.

# Increase Trust and Oxytocin

**You will be happier when trust and bonding chemicals are released.**

When you start sharing your hobbies and passions at work, you'll feel physical changes. There's a tingling in your brain thanks to two chemicals in particular that are released: norepinephrine and oxytocin.

Norepinephrine is released when you come across something unique. Maybe it's best explained using the phrase, "You're interested in interesting things." And the more attracted and interested we are, the more it's released. When I'm speaking at an event to a room full of professionals, if I learn that someone is a scuba diver, or if I learn somebody plays the guitar, or if I learn somebody volunteers at an animal shelter, norepinephrine is released. Scientists have found this makes us feel giddy, energetic, alert, and euphoric—all of which enhance our abilities at work.

And right there with norepinephrine is oxytocin. Studies show that your brain releases more oxytocin during positive social interactions and social contact, such as taking the time to talk with someone about an interesting topic.

Could the interesting topic be work-related? Possibly. Could the interesting topic also be unrelated to work? Definitely.

That's why I encourage everyone to have normal conversations with others as often as possible. When I talked with Steve Browne, he suggested people get out from behind their desks and go talk to the people they work with.

> Your desk is your enemy. Unless there are people surrounding your desk like a giant beehive, people are not in your office. Get out of your office and see people. If you need that structure, put time in your schedule. Block time out to, say, take fifteen minutes one day a week to talk to John. If John goes, "Hey man, I'm good." At least it was blocked out and I was intentional about it.
>
> I think the other thing is to fight your biases. We tend to hang out with people we like and the people we don't like, we talk about, which is not cool. I think you have to be an equal opportunity liker.
>
> **STEVE BROWNE** MUSIC LOVER

It's easy to come up with excuses for why we can't get out from behind our desk and talk to others. They're not in the same building as you? Then do a video call. Why? Because oxytocin leads to trust and bonding—two things that are absolutely critical for doing your best work. Without trust and bonding, engagement doesn't exist and turnover is sure to be high.

Other benefits from oxytocin include becoming more relaxed, empathetic, cooperative, and extroverted—all characteristics that make for a great professional. It also reduces your body's release of cortisol so you'll have less stress and anxiety. It's a little difficult to do your best work when your stress and anxiety levels are through the roof.

You'll know if this bonding has happened when you have a big project that requires long hours, like during busy season for tax professionals, when times get tough, or when you're working a lot of overtime to meet deadlines. If you've taken the time before that crunch to encourage activities that release oxytocin, your lows won't be so low. You've developed trust and bonded with your colleagues, so you know you're in this with people who have a genuine interest in each other and you have a genuine interest in them. That's when oxytocin pulls you together.

I'd like to add that "trusted advisor" is a phrase that seems to be very popular now, with companies and firms putting it on their business cards and websites. But unless there's oxytocin released between you and a client, you can't call yourself a "trusted advisor"—because there's no trust. And unless you're having normal conversations with people at work, then there's no oxytocin. In order to make this easier, you're going to want norepinephrine released, which can only happen if you're interesting.

*If you truly want to call yourself a "trusted advisor," you're going to have to be interesting.*

If you're a super professional who got 100 percent on all your exams in college and you have every certification, know these achievements alone aren't enough for people to trust you. Being technically proficient doesn't always translate into the ability to build a relationship. It takes having natural conversations with others to build that trust and bonding. I realize it's not inherent to a lot of professionals to have these conversations at work, but a little bit of humanity goes a long way toward the release of oxytocin and norepinephrine.

# Fulfillment Is Not Generational

**We all want to be more fulfilled, no matter our age.**

Some people might think that happiness and fulfillment at work is a generational thing, something millennials came up with. But this isn't a millennial thing: it's a human thing. Every single one of us wants to be understood and appreciated by those around us. Everyone I've talked to willingly accepts this new emphasis on happiness and fulfillment—even if they're a little disgruntled that it wasn't the same way when they were younger. People understand that flexibility to spend time with family or on other interests makes for a more positive and productive workplace. After adopting this philosophy, people are more energized and bring a unique perspective to their jobs.

And regardless of your age, it's been shown that you don't need to wait until retirement to engage in your outside-of-work passions. Do them now!

# PART 4

## Sharing Interests Deepens the Relationships Among Employees

# The Connections Pyramid

**True connections with others happen when you move from work to play.**

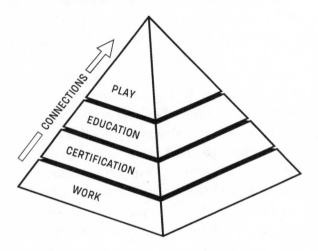

There are many ways we connect with others at work. The bottom layer in the illustration above, which represents the weakest connection, represents how you're connected to the people you work with simply because you all work for the same company or organization. If you see someone with a logo-emblazoned golf shirt or computer bag, you automatically have a connection with them that goes above and beyond what you'd have with another stranger.

At the office, you meet someone who has your same niche technical expertise. You learn this from the certification hanging on the wall or the letters after their name on their business card, which designate some sort of expertise. Odds are good that you spend a lot of time with that person because you're both working on the projects specific to that expertise.

Then you might come across someone who went to the same school you did. Maybe it's the degree hanging on the wall or the apparel they wear on casual Fridays or you heard them talking about the school's sports teams. You are instantly good friends, even though you never met at school. That common experience creates a stronger bond than with others at your company, especially if there are sports rivalries to talk about. In my experience, this common bond trumps any other work-related bond.

And that's where the old model of professionalism stops. The answer to the question, "What do you do?" is covered in the first three levels of the pyramid: "I work at XYZ company, attended XYZ school, and have XYZ designations." That's a safe answer, which is easily verified with certificates and degrees. You may think this is all the information someone needs to know or even cares to know about you: "No need to creep them out by sharing too much about myself. Where I went to college is personal enough."

But there's another level to the pyramid, the top level, where connections are strongest. That connection is *play*. These are your passions and interests outside of work. These are the passions that enhance the bottom three layers. These are the interests that truly connect you to others and the passions that people genuinely care about. If you were to meet someone who is avid about the same outside-of-work interest as you, your connection with them will be stronger than any of the connections you have at the other layers.

> People say, "You're the CEO, you're the owner, you can't be friends with your team." I've said, "Well, you know what, I just don't believe that." It's my responsibility to hire the right people, and then to give them the opportunity to learn about each other and have a connection outside of work … I mean, what if you are a Giants football fan and somebody else is a Giants fan? Now you have a buddy and now you're going to team up against the Green Bay guy, and on Sunday you're going to have something to talk about. Or what if you're like, "My kids in dance." And they're like, "Oh yeah? That's great, I was just thinking about putting my daughter in dance. Can you give me any recommendations?"
>
> **DAWN BROLIN** SOFTBALL PLAYER/COACH

And even if your outside-of-work passion is unique—like me doing comedy—the play level will still bring everyone closer together. Coworkers are able to have a genuine interest in those around them, as opposed to just knowing what their job is. As you move up the pyramid, your connections with others get stronger. It's nearly impossible for anyone to know, like, or trust you unless you are willing to get to the play level of the pyramid.

But the traditional sense of professionalism tells us that not only does the play level not matter but no one even cares about that. I hope that you now see this is completely untrue. Perhaps the next time someone asks, "What do you do?" your answer will include your "And." Professionals should care about those around them to the point that sharing these passions and interests becomes an integral part of doing business.

# Twelve Years Later...

**Does sharing the real you help
you stand out? You better believe it!**

I didn't realize how much of an impact that sharing your passions and interests has on others until I was speaking at a relatively large event in Houston. As I was backstage going over my notes, the meeting planner approached, gave me the name of one of the conference attendees, and asked me if I knew him. When I told her that I had never heard that name in my life, she said, "Well, he knows you. He saw the list of speakers and right away said, 'I know John Garrett! That's the guy who did comedy at night.'"

Later that evening, I decided to do a little digging to find this guy. I came to find out that he was in the tax department at my first PwC office in St. Louis. I'm 100 percent positive we never worked together, because despite having an accounting degree, I have very little knowledge of how taxes work. And I'm 99 percent positive that we have never met.

I was floored to realize that it had been at least twelve years since I had worked at PwC, yet I'm on a short list of people that he immediately recalls? And for nothing work-related? I had put in a lot of time to have a strong résumé, yet he doesn't remember me for my degree or my certification. Instead, he recalled that I had started my hobby doing amateur stand-up at comedy club open mic nights—which has nothing to do with accounting at all!

So, I'll ask you: What is it that you are doing today that will make your clients and coworkers remember you twelve years from now? I promise you the answer isn't work-related—provided you don't burn down the building holding your red Swingline stapler, like Milton did in *Office Space*. If you don't give them something to remember by sharing your outside-of-work interests, it's very possible you'll be forgotten altogether. And you're too good at what you do and work way too hard for them not to remember you.

Everyone deserves to have someone remember them twelve years later.

## PART 5

# Sharing Interests Enhances Your Career

# Free Time You
# Is the Real You

**Don't hinder your career by hiding your passions.**

Once we leave work, we can do whatever we want. This is our free time. The time to do what we want, how we want, and for as long as we want. Until the next business day starts anyway.

What you do with this time demonstrates the real you. These are the passions that drive you. You're probably not making any money from these hobbies. More than likely, you're paying to participate in them.

No matter what your passion is, the reason you work is to make money so you can go do cool things. We work so we can live. Sure, you might be good at your job, but you can't wait to go do that outside-of-work passion.

And you might just discover how much that passion helps your career.

> One of the things that you and I discussed in our first conversation, which honestly has led me to such a life "aha moment" was how much theater was influencing my career and the choices I was making—decisions regarding conferences and all of these other things that had production or marketing elements. And so I asked myself, "Why am I separating my art and my career, and why aren't I blending that more?"

**MISTY MEGIA** THEATER DIRECTOR/CHOREOGRAPHER

# Stand Out from Your Peers

**Your passions make you unique and memorable compared to your colleagues.**

I remember my first day at PwC, meeting everyone else in my start class. On paper, we were all identical—accounting degree from an accredited university and preparing to sit for the CPA exam. But we were all so completely different from each other in personality and interests outside of work.

There's no doubt that the same is true where you work. You are surrounded by professionals who have very similar degrees and certifications. And yet there's no doubt in my mind that you and your colleagues are all unique. Not because of the degrees and certifications—those are almost identical for everyone. Your uniqueness comes from your life experiences and passions outside of work. It's these life experiences and passions combined with your technical skills that you—and only you—bring to your job. No one else in your profession, and definitely not in your organization, has the same combination you have.

It's funny because I keep [my model ships] in my cubicle area. I have anywhere between six and ten. They're—how do I put it?—the magic show that doesn't stop performing. Since they're just out there, people stop. They're coming to ask me questions or for whatever they need. They're like, "Oh my goodness. Did you build these?" "Yes, I did." Then a conversation just starts on its own. I don't really have to bring it up that much, but it's always a great conversation starter.

**DANIEL SIEMENS**  SHIP IN BOTTLE BUILDER

Whenever I go to a new client office, I always ask them, "What do you do?" They typically answer with something about their job. I stop them and say, "No, no, I already know that. What do you do outside of work?" I genuinely care about what makes each person unique and this provides something interesting to make the relationship "sticky."

# Help Your Company Stand Out

### How to find your true differentiator.

When a client is looking to have a tax return done, or get some legal advice, or find some help for their business, it can be overwhelming to see how many professionals offer the service they need. They all seem the same. And in many cases, they are exactly the same. So, what makes a client choose you or your organization over another?

Whenever I ask an executive what makes their organization unique, the answer is always "the people!" But what is it about the people that is unique?

In almost every instance, it isn't the technical expertise—it's their personalities and passions outside of work. If I were to replace everyone from your department with people who had the same degrees, certifications, and technical skills, the end work product would be the same—but it would be a completely different department.

I call this the Culture Core. Why? Because each individual is unique and brings a unique perspective to the job. And those unique individuals can make your organization stand out from the rest!

Around Christmastime, I made some homemade cookies for some clients and also custom BeachFleischman chocolate-covered Oreos. They seemed to like them. I'm trying to spend some more time on that, probably after busy season, and getting those custom Oreos out to the clients. I'd like to have them available in the office for us to give out to our clients when they come in because I think that really helps us stand out. It's only a cookie, but when you talk to your friend about your CPA who gave you cookies, they'll be like, "Oh, I need to go to that CPA."

**ASHLEY BYMA** CAKE DECORATOR

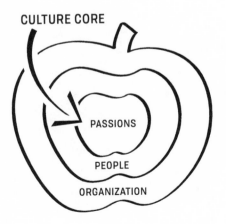

It's only natural to conclude that the very core of your organization's culture is your people's outside-of-work hobbies and passions. It's what makes your organization unique; it's what allows you to bring a different level of service to your clients. Each person's individuality is undoubtedly the core of your culture.

Those executives I asked are right; it is "the people." But even more specifically than that, it's their outside-of-work passions and interests.

# The Path to
# New Clients

**Through your passions, you will discover new business opportunities—because it's easy for a conversation to go from personal to business.**

I've heard countless stories from people who have developed new business opportunities through their hobby or passion. For instance, MB Raimondi started making stained glass art at a studio. A few months later, that studio became her newest bookkeeping client.

> I like to share information with clients. And certainly, when I'm out teaching, to make it personal to connect with the audience or to connect with my clients, I think it's important to be kind of open and share yourself. In that respect, the fact that I'll talk about stained glass, I think it humanizes me. It takes me more out of the green eyeshade accountant and [leads clients to] say, "Wow, this woman has a life outside of accounting," which it sounds as—you know, it's pretty cool.
>
> **MB RAIMONDI** STAINED GLASS ARTIST

Had they not explored their hobbies or passions, these people wouldn't have made these business contacts. Going to networking events can lead to new business—but not if you only talk work. Everyone else at that event is talking about the same thing and you quickly become a commodity with no real way of standing out or being memorable. And if you're part of a pitch to get a new client, you can use your organization's personality and outside-of-work passions to stand out from your competition. In almost every instance, you and your competition are relatively similar when it comes to technical skills. In order to stand out, you need something else.

Exploring your passions as a business development tool is something that you may or may not eventually learn. And if you do, it'll probably be by accident. I've asked everyone I've interviewed if they learned this in business school and the answer has always been no. I also ask them if they learned this in their professional continuing education and the answer has always been no. But this is a skill that is critical to your success, so I believe it should be taught early and reinforced often.

I have found that it's much easier to introduce your passions early in a conversation with someone. Not only does it develop rapport with the other person and create a connection on a deeper level than simply talking about work, but it's also much smoother to take a conversation from personal to work than the other way around. If you lead with talking about work, you'll have a much more difficult time transitioning to outside-of-work interests.

# Best Versus Different

**Be different and watch the opportunities roll in.**

While many professionals think they are playing it safe by going unnoticed, this has proven not to be a good career strategy; you're more likely to get passed over for promotions and not included on the projects you'd enjoy most. Unless you work for an organization that simply "promotes who's left," then you're going to have to be noticed at some point. In Seth Godin's book *Purple Cow*, he writes, "If you're not standing out, then you're completely invisible." I believe this applies to both individuals and organizations. Professionals should be encouraged to stand out and understand that being invisible isn't an option.

I believe there are two ways to stand out—you can be the best or you can be different.

We are all trained to try to be the best. All through school, it's stressed that we need to master the technical skills in order to get good grades. Then we get the job and our employer continues to train us with technical skills so we can be the best at our job.

And every organization tries to say that they are the best. For clients. And for talent.

The big problem with this is: Who defines "best"? What you consider to be the best may not be what I consider to be the best. This played out perfectly one time when I was on stage at an event in Austin, Texas. I asked the audience who the best software implementer was in the room and one consultant boldly raised her hand.

After finding out her name and where she was from, I then asked her, "So you think you're the best? What makes you the best?"

"My years of experience—seventeen years is a long time," she told me.

"Just out of curiosity, has anyone here been implementing the software for longer than seventeen years?" I asked.

Another consultant raised her hand as she shouted, "Twenty-three years!"

That's when I turned to the first person who had spoken up and jokingly said, "Uh-oh. I guess you're not the best anymore!"

Clearly, they were both good at what they do. You don't have a career that long if you're terrible at your job. But being the best is ruthless. Best only allows for one "winner." You're playing musical chairs with an infinite number of players and there's only one chair. I don't know about you, but I don't like those odds.

I found out the first consultant had her private pilot's license. Wow! That's so much more interesting to talk about than "years of service." Not only that, if she's pitching for work at an airport, or any business related to building aircraft, or to a decision-maker who is also a pilot, I'm sure that she would be considered the best. She understands the industry on a much deeper level thanks to her outside-of-work passion.

Best can be beaten by being different. And different isn't ruthless. Different allows for everyone to stand out.

> Your work product is assumed to be great. And that's not to be arrogant. It's just to get to this level, you have to do that kind of work, right? So, the assumption is that it's going to be really good. So, to differentiate yourself that way is really difficult. And you know what? It's almost like the frog in the boiling water pan. Your clients internally just... assume that it's easy for you and you're no longer special. You're just another one of those really good lawyers.
>
> To have something that they can talk to you about or you can talk to folks about that has nothing to do with the work product, has nothing to do with the case, I think it's refreshing on both sides. At least it seems to have played

out in my favor. I've seen that there are several others of us who, what I like to say, bring our whole self to work. Those folks tend to have better relationships in the office, and it seems to work out well for them.

**SHANNON PETERS** GUITARIST

# Something to Look Forward to When You Retire

**Don't be the person who leaves the workplace with nothing to live for. Or doesn't leave at all.**

Retirement might seem like something so far in the future that you can't even think about it. But the truth is that at some point you're going to either stop working or work less than you did when you were younger. What will fill that time?

As a consultant, I've had discussions with several executives who are within five years of retirement and they've admitted they don't know how they're going to spend their time. One was a partner at an international consulting firm. After hearing me speak, he realized he had spent so much time building his career that he had forgotten that he once had outside-of-work interests. And now that he's nearing retirement age, he was a little worried about how he would occupy his time.

How scary is that? Imagine you've had a successful career, have more money than you need, have all the time in the world—but you don't have any idea what to do with all that hard-earned time and money. Staying true to your passions outside of work allows you to not only be happier in the present but be happier in the future. Plus, having that hobby waiting for you will encourage you to develop new leaders so you can actually retire, instead of continuing to work forever.

I also believe that having no activities outside of the office is one of the leading reasons for the lack of succession planning in organizations. Because the corporate leaders are so consumed with their jobs, they haven't taken the time to nurture any outside-of-work passions. This means they have nothing to look forward to once they retire, so they push off retirement for as long as possible. Their whole identity is wrapped up in their work. It's very possible that the only thing that will stop these individuals from working is death. Right there in their office chair. Or maybe it's the required retirement age in their partnership agreement that forces them to leave. Most professionals have no interest in working themselves to death—literally—and are definitely not interested in working for an organization with a "work till you drop because what else is there?" culture!

At some point, leadership needs to hand over the reins. It's in the best interests of the company and its customers or clients that leaders are available to provide guidance for a smooth transition.

During your career, you will have many transitions. You need to make sure that you are prepared to retire and live your new life filled with hobbies and passions. The more you explore these passions while you are working, the smoother the transition will be at the end of your career.

MODULE

2

# DON'T BE AFRAID!

# *Don't Be Afraid...* Even If This May Not Be Easy

By now you know that I'm asking you to stand out, to be yourself, to let the whole you come to work. For a lot of people, this won't be easy because everything I'm telling you goes against everything you've been taught since you were little. When we were kids, anyone who stood out was different or odd; they were made fun of until they conformed to what the majority thought was normal. Oftentimes, professionalism encourages organizations to reinforce this belief that conforming is safest. Except we aren't kids anymore. We're adults. And standing out can be advantageous.

Why do I say this isn't going to be easy? Because it's human nature to avoid being vulnerable. And as a professional, it's in your nature to always know the answer and to always be correct. But you don't always have to know all the answers; you only need to know who does know the answers.

You've no doubt worked really hard to earn your degree and get those certifications. And because you spent so much time in pursuit of degrees and accreditations, it's easy to feel that they are a bigger part of your identity than they actually are. Too many professionals let their work identity become their entire identity—even when they're outside of work.

In addition, this work identity is the one that pays the bills and the mortgage and allows you to do the things that you love to do. So it's natural for professionals to feel that the technical skills they've learned are the most important things they know.

It's also difficult because professionalism hasn't always allowed for individuality or for people to share their hobbies and passions in the workplace. A lot of organizations have spent a lot of time hammering everyone flat so that no one stands out. It's definitely easier for management to look at staff as a "group of professionals" with the same characteristics. This is further exacerbated when younger professionals see more advanced staff, managers, and executives all behaving in a certain way; they tend to imitate that behavior to conform.

> It's just about knowing really, truly for yourself what it is that you're about and what you're interested in—that is step one. And test the waters. Find where the line is. Have faith and trust that they have hired you for you. Don't think you have to fit this weird cookie-cutter mold. Each of us are different and we're each bringing something unique to the table and that's a valuable thing.
>
> **LAUREN THIEL** HIP-HOP DANCER

Others used to have an interest outside of work but, due to the stress of their work, family life, or their commute, they don't feel they have the energy to pursue those interests anymore. It's important to note that this is completely normal. Your hobby or outside-of-work interest doesn't need to be done on a daily or even monthly basis. But it's crucial that you intentionally set aside time to pursue your passions and interests. It could be as simple as a quarterly bike ride or an annual walk for charity.

After hearing me speak at a conference, the executive vice president of a software company admitted that she hadn't gone running in years. She used to run several times a week, but work started taking up more of her time. "I kept telling myself that I would just run next week. It seems that has turned into a few years!" she told me. "That hadn't dawned on me until you just brought it up." Make time for what's important to you outside of work or your passions will go dormant and eventually extinct—you may not even remember what you were once interested in.

I'm here to tell you not to be afraid because so many people have shared their "And" before you, including me. In my research, I have found that most people's fear of talking about their interests isn't based in reality—

it's only in their heads. When they share their hobbies and passions with others in the workplace, they find that the reaction is much more positive than they predicted. Provided your passion doesn't involve you doing anything illegal, I'm confident the same thing will happen for you.

It's completely okay for you to be a little anxious, but don't ever be afraid because you should know you aren't alone. You've got me. You've also got every single guest who has ever been on the *What's Your "And"?* podcast. And you've got the 92 percent of professionals who also admit to having an outside-of-work hobby or passion.

## *Don't Be Afraid to...*
# Interact Outside the Office

The easiest way to get to know the people with whom you work is to spend time together outside of the office. For some reason, when people enter their workplaces, they leave a part of themselves outside. It's critical that you coordinate activities where you can get to know each other on a different level. It can be as simple as going out to lunch or taking a walk. You can also invite someone to do an activity with you or invite a group of people to come to your show.

From experience, I know that it can be nerve-racking to invite people from work to watch you perform. When coworkers came to see me at a comedy show, I was certainly more nervous than if they had not been there. But even if it wasn't my best set, they were still excited to be there, to support me, and to see me in my element. That meant so much to me and led to stronger connections at work.

Why is it that everyone on your softball team knows you are an accountant or lawyer or engineer, but no one in your office knows you're a softball player? Don't be afraid to not only share your hobby or passion with someone by talking about it in the office but go ahead and invite them to be a part of it as well.

# *Don't Be Afraid to...* Have Items in Your Office That Declare Your Passion

One of the easiest ways to show people that you have passions and interests outside of work is to display small things in your cubicle or office or on your computer desktop wallpaper. Not only do these items bring you joy but they also spark conversation with others.

Chris Morrison has often hiked in Grand Canyon and Zion National Parks and has taken some amazing pictures on these adventures. He displays some of these photos in his office, and several times they have led to conversations and even surprise that they were taken by Chris himself.

> I try to decorate my office with photos that I've actually taken on my hikes. People come in all the time and say, "Oh, that's a really cool new photo you got." Once they realize that I took it, a conversation breaks out and people get to know me. The next thing I know, I have people who are walking by my office stop in occasionally and ask me what I did this past weekend or what my plan is for next weekend.
>
> **CHRIS MORRISON** ADVENTURE PHOTOGRAPHER

Something this simple can lead to stronger connections and more interesting conversations that will in turn lead to deeper relationships.

Bring in your artwork, concert posters, or pictures of the car you just remodeled. Not only will your workplace be more enjoyable if you surround yourself with what reminds you of these passions that light you up, but you'll have more interesting conversations with everyone around you.

# *Don't Be Afraid to...*
# Fight This on a Daily Basis

This is a battle. And it's very real. And it happens daily. Many people have been indoctrinated with this false definition of a "professional" for so long that it's very difficult for us—and those around us—not to slip back into our old belief that we must pretend we're not multidimensional.

This regression can happen when times are stressful and you have a lot of work to do. Your instinct might be to laser focus on work so you can get it completed. While this is obviously important, it's just as important not to forget the human side of everyone around you. Successful professionals know that talking about outside-of-work interests can inject some energy and engagement into the team.

This regression can also happen when we compare our outside-of-work interests with others'. You might not run a marathon as fast as someone else in your office, but you're still a runner. Your art might not be hanging in a gallery, but you're still an artist. I've found that we are particularly critical of ourselves and have a difficult time identifying ourselves with a label that applies to our passions or interests. To make this easier, start by saying, "I enjoy running" or "I enjoy painting."

That's something that anyone can say with confidence because it doesn't matter how good someone else thinks you are, you're doing that hobby or passion for yourself.

> I will tell you I have never done anything in my life that is more of a confidence booster than being on a motorcycle. You get off and you go, "Look what I've done," and of course the speed and the smell of the gas and the engine is wonderful and you get off and the adrenaline rush is phenomenal. And whenever I race, for the next month or two, it's like there's nothing I can't do.
>
> **REBECCA BERNECK** MOTORCYCLE RACER

Take solace in the fact that having multiple dimensions means you are in the majority and you are the norm. Don't feel pressured to hide your outside-of-work self while you're using your technical expertise to do your job.

# *Don't Be Afraid to...* Take a Genuine Interest in Others

It's imperative that you take a genuine interest in others at work. The key word there is "genuine."

A great question to ask, even during interviews, is, "What do you love to do when you aren't working?" Once one of you starts talking about your outside-of-work interests, the universe will feel out of balance so the other person will feel compelled to share, too. This reciprocity allows you to build deeper relationships if you're willing to open up as well.

If you are in a leadership position, it's imperative that you encourage this. Try modeling this behavior so your team sees that you truly believe it's okay. Most professionals seek permission and want to play it safe for fear of being reprimanded. It's great if you tell people it's okay to share their hobbies and interests, but it's always best if you show them. Get out from behind your desk and spend time getting to know the people you work with. And even if you're reluctant to share yourself, don't ever discourage the team from sharing their hobbies and passions with each other. As long as the work is being done and deadlines are being met, no one should be made to feel guilty for pursuing their outside-of-work passions.

My first full-time gig was the summer of the 2008 Olympics, which I'm sure all of you have marked on your calendars and remember so fondly like us swimmers do. There was this new swimsuit technology that had come out in the prior years, which—we won't get too technical, but—helped swimmers go faster because they were basically floating on top of the water. I'm this twenty-one-year-old kid in this big office environment with all these other people starting at the same time. A lot of people were coming up to me—partners included and local leaders in the office here in DC—and they'd say, "Tell me more about these swimsuits. What's going on?" I got some good face time out of it, which turned into some good stories and some good contacts I have to this day.

**CHRIS EKIMOFF** SWIMMER

# Don't Be Afraid to...
# Make It Easy for Someone
# to Go Second

The second person to share is always the most essential. While it's important that you share your hobbies and passions, it's equally important for you to make it safe and easy for the next person to share, too. Why? Because if you're the only one sharing, it definitely won't become part of your organization's culture.

In the same way that an event has to repeat for more than one year for it to be called an annual tradition, it takes more than one person doing something for it to be considered normal. Sharing first encourages others to share their outside-of-work passions, and keeping up the momentum is key. Remember, we aren't talking about the kind of sharing that's disruptive or inappropriate, but rather we're trying to get to know one another on a deeper level.

Each person decides how much they want to share based on their comfort level. Therefore, it's important that the first person who shares makes it safe and even encourages the second person to share, in their own way. By accepting each person's comfort level and continuing to create a safe and welcoming environment, the group will self-regulate as others join them.

By continuing in this manner, people create stronger bonds. Normalizing this behavior also contributes to what eventually is part of the culture.

> Why not just be yourself? Because, honestly, once we can share what makes us different, then we can see what makes us the same. And I think that it's really important to be brave; I say "be brave" because somebody has to go first and it's not often the first person that makes the biggest impact, it's the second person. The first person makes it safe, but the second person is crucial to making this normal. As more people continue to share, they make it safer and before you know it, everyone else is doing it, too.
>
> **PHIL GERBYSHAK** PINBALL WIZARD

# *Don't Be Afraid to...*
# Be Vulnerable

Many professionals feel that keeping their passions to themselves is the safest move and best for their career development. They feel that talking about them will make them vulnerable and others will perceive them as not being very good at their job.

These professionals are wrong. Dead wrong. If you want to be staffed on a cool project, the manager needs to know who you are. Otherwise, you're playing roulette in hopes they pick you. If all they know about you is your degree and certifications—the exact same ones that most of your peers have—then you aren't going to stand out.

In the same way, if you want to be promoted, executives need to know who you are. If you want to grow your business, clients need to know who you are.

The odds of this happening are a bit slim if you keep your outside-of-work interests hidden.

Not only is it okay to be vulnerable, it's absolutely vital as a professional.

Every year, my firm throws a party at a big hospitality suite for a lot of their friends and clients in one of the major industries that we service down in Atlantic City. We had rented out a restaurant and we were going to have a five-hour hors d'oeuvre passing and open bar kind of thing for everybody. As the new guy and as the marketing guy, I guess I drew the short straw and was assigned to do all the logistics for it. [On the night of the event] I got to the space and set everything up. I was bracing myself before we began and I saw they had a great big grand piano on the stage and I asked the staff, "Hey, we've got like fifteen to twenty minutes before we get this whole show on the road. Do you mind if I just noodle here for a little while?" And they were like, "Yeah, go ahead, whatever."

Five hours later, I was still there. Yeah, I sat down and I just started noodling and my partners, as they were coming in, were like, "Hey, just keep doing that," and the clients and everybody really loved it ... We'll be doing the event again and this time, I'll actually bring music!

**JEFF CROSLEY** PIANIST

# *Don't Be Afraid to ...*
# Nourish the Whole Person

When you hire someone, you are hiring the whole person. You're not just hiring the technical skills—the part that knows how to do the job. I was once talking with an executive and he said that he always makes sure that his people are happy with their outside-of-work lives. When I asked him why that was so important, he said that in his career, he's never seen anyone be productive and engaged at work when their outside-of-work life is out of balance.

I know a lot of organizations provide training and continuing education to their employees to sharpen their technical skills so they can do their jobs better. It's great to develop your people and invest in them, but you've got to allow them to invest in and develop other aspects of their lives as well.

It's important to remember to shine a light on those things that people do outside the office. It's crucial to not only allow them to do those things on a regular basis but to celebrate with them. Ask how her mountain bike race was. Ask how his painting is coming along. Ask how her vacation was. And ask to see pictures and hear stories about their interests outside of work.

Do these activities have anything to do with the end product at work? Probably not. Do these activities have a charge code to account for your time? No. Do these activities make work better and easier? Absolutely.

Showing a genuine interest in the people around you helps create a culture where people want to be more engaged and more productive—and more likely to stay longer at your organization. By showing that you care about other aspects of someone's life, you're creating a stronger relationship that can withstand critical feedback.

# *Don't Be Afraid to...*
# Acknowledge That
# People Work to Live

The sooner we admit that we're working so we can live, the sooner things will improve in your team's level of engagement. We work to be productive, but we also work to earn money to be able to do what we're passionate about. Being good at your job doesn't make it your true passion in life. And if someone has passions outside of work, that doesn't mean they are bad at their job.

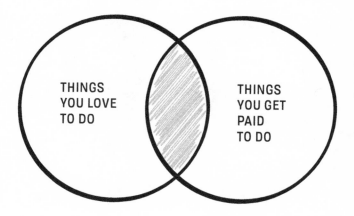

Sure, there are some parts of your job that you love to do but rarely does someone love *all* of them. And that's a natural part of work.

Your outside-of-work passions don't earn you any money and you often pay to do them. Would you do your job if you had to pay money to do it? People often laugh in my face when I ask them that. If you were thinking, "Heck, no, John!" then your work is clearly not your passion. No doubt you're good at what you do, because you're still getting paid, but there's something else that has your interest.

> My mom used to always say, and I constantly think about it, that you work to live, not live to work. Not that there's anything wrong with work, but if you're thinking your job is who you are, and your value and your worth is connected completely to your job, then that's a problem because when tasks change or your circumstances change, that can actually undermine you and your thinking about yourself.

**CLAYTON OATES** WORLD TRAVELER

Your hobby doesn't have to be anything over-the-top amazing. I recently spoke at a CFO conference and there was a CFO who went scuba diving in the Red Sea and another who was on a competitive roller derby team—which are both super cool! Afterward, I was talking to some of the other audience members who felt that their passions weren't as exciting. Don't ever judge your passion against someone else's. You're not doing it for them—you're doing it for you. There's probably a greater likelihood that someone else you work with does the same thing as you. And if so, are you going to tell them their hobby is boring? Of course not, so get to sharing already.

# *Don't Be Afraid to...*
# Apply Skills Developed
# Outside Work to Your Job

Many of the people I've interviewed have been able to develop and sharpen skills that can be used at work. These people's skills and talents differ from others who might have the same education or certification. If you know that someone excels at some technical skill, you'd maximize that talent. There's no difference when it comes to skills developed outside of work. It's important to understand that people have these skills and to find ways to let them use them.

> The biggest challenge with the sport [of curling] is there's really no individual—you're only as good as the weakest link. In a lot of sports, you can be carried by the best players. In curling, you can't have that. It really takes all four members to get it right and it only takes one to mess it up. [As the rock is sliding], you have to know who's calling what, who's yelling what, and why, and you all have to get on the same page quickly.
>
> That's a real metaphor for work, I guess, that you're all part of the team. You have to work together and you all rely on each other not only to do your job but to not mess up anyone else's job. And the communication is often the hardest because plans change—you call a shot and you

might think that you're all doing this, but halfway down something happens and you need to change your mind. If you had four people in a room and you quickly had to change the plan while stuff was happening, could you efficiently communicate it so that everyone would know that you'd changed your mind?

**PAUL MEISSNER** CURLER

# *Don't Be Afraid to...*
## Be More Relatable

At the very least, sharing your interests makes you relatable. This is especially important as you continue to get promoted and take on leadership positions. I think it's easy to forget that younger staff look at an executive or partner in awe. You're like a fictional character that they've seen in movies and TV shows who has a corner office and is unapproachable. By sharing the human side of you, it shows everyone that it's okay to have interests outside of work. But more importantly, it makes you relatable. It would be amazing if someone else you work with has the same passion. But if not, they can still look at you as an interesting person with a first name, instead of a cookie-cutter authority figure with a title. Instead of going to talk to the partner or CMO, staff can go talk to Brenda or Tom.

> I'm uncertain when Disney came into my life as it seems to have always been a part of it, but now it's all I want to do. It's just sunny there and people at Disney World are always in a good mood. It's definitely my happy place! More and more, I just realized that life is too short and as nerdy as your passion is, you need to embrace it and just not really care what people are going to think of you. I'll spend time talking to colleagues or clients and find out

different things that they like, and a lot of times they do like Disney as well, which is nice to have this common bond.

**CINDY SCHROEDER** DISNERD

# *Don't Be Afraid to...*
## Be an Original

When we start our first corporate job, we naturally model the behavior of those around us. We have certain ideas of how someone should behave in that profession and we morph ourselves, a little or a lot, to fit that mold.

As we get promoted, we do this even more by modeling the behavior of those above us. But what you don't realize is that those people are modeling the behavior of those before them, who are modeling their behavior on those before them, and so on. Somewhere long ago, I guess there was someone so consumed with his job and everyone unwittingly copied him.

Not being your authentic self at work is a disservice to you, your organization, and anyone looking up to you. The company hired *you*. A few years later, the company promoted *you*. The best thing you can do is be *you* at work. Not a copy of a copy of what you think is a "professional."

The world is starving for authenticity and uniqueness. There are already enough people working at your organization who are trying hard to behave the same way. Don't fall into that trap.

We have so many things to prove. Especially being a person of color, we're brought up thinking, "Oh, I've got to prove to everybody that I got the job, I earned it, and I'm qualified to do it." Sometimes, letting people in and seeing the person is a scary thing to do when you really are trying to say, "Let me just give you my credentials. Let me show you how I can help you … Yoga and martial arts really teach you how to do that. How to stop, how to slow down, how to take a deep breath and focus on what's in front of you, what's right there, that person who's right there. I think, as a result, I actually started taking time to get to know people better. And they felt that they got to know me better, instead of just thinking, "Well, Ivy's a consummate professional," which is what many people would say. But that doesn't say anything about who Ivy is as a person other than her persona and how she might deal with you.

**IVY ANDERSON** PHOTOGRAPHER/TAE KWON DO BLACK BELT

# *Don't Be Afraid to...*
# Take the Initiative

The great news is that this change can happen from anywhere in the organization. Take me for example. When I was at PwC, there wasn't a directive or a formal program for everyone to share their hobbies. I just did it among my small circle of peers or with others working with me on a client project. When someone asked me how my weekend was, I would tell them what comedy club show I had done.

The top-down approach does make it easier. If an organization's leaders display this behavior—encouraging people to share their outside-of-work interests—then it gives everyone permission to do the same. And the byproduct of that is a more approachable leadership group with more engaged employees who stay longer.

I think it's a trickle-down effect. Whatever [attitude] is at the top of the firm tends to trickle down. I had somebody recently say to me, "You, Twyla, inspired me to start running again," and that was because I started to share a few more posts on social media about my running. I feel honored to be able to do that for somebody. [Upper-level managers should be] sharing and creating that environment where maybe you take every Monday morning, and you just have a fifteen-minute around-the-coffee-pot and ask who did what and what happened—or [any exchange] that's just something a bit more relaxed where you don't feel the pressure of the time commitments that we all have as professionals to get something out the door. Actually take a moment to just be with the people who you work with and get to know them a bit better.

**TWYLA VERHELST** MARATHONER

That being said, it's still on the individual to participate. The organization's leaders can only do so much to create the culture and a safe environment for everyone to share. But they can't force you to do it. No matter where you are on the organizational chart, take the initiative.

# *Don't Be Afraid to...* Let People Do Their Extracurricular Activities

The sooner we all admit that we enjoy extracurricular activities, the sooner we can create a more positive workplace. As my research shows, nearly everyone has something they love to do outside of work. Oftentimes, people are hired because they have interesting extracurricular activities, such as being part of a sports team or a nonprofit group. Some organizations forget this and don't give their people time to do these activities and are left puzzled at why engagement is so low and turnover is so high. Maybe, just maybe, it's because leaders aren't embracing the whole person—the person with technical skills *and* outside-of-work interests. Remember this isn't an either/or situation. It's both/and. People have their work life *and* their outside-of-work life; they should never be forced to choose just one part of their identity.

> I think our firm is becoming a refuge for the accountants who have something going on in their lives outside of the office. I'm talking like top of their league, the rock stars of their firms. But they're coming to us going, "Hey, I want to come over because my firm takes issue with the fact

that I do [blank]." That could be modeling. That could be dancing. That could be a professional skater, a professional wrestler, in a band, et cetera. I've heard these stories where the partners have sat this person down and go, "Look. About the band, yeah. I saw what you did, posting it on Instagram, and we don't think that's becoming of a professional." Imagine the audacity to single out a top performer in your firm and say, "Look. You're a good performer in the office and we want to keep you but you have to quit this thing." That is not a conversation that you should be having because ultimately what happens is, they end up leaving because that outside-of-work passion is really important.

**CHRIS HOOPER** WEIGHTLIFTER

Sure, there is work to be done. And certain times of the year might be a lot busier than others, so work takes priority as we get our tasks completed. But studies have shown that better work is done by people who are happier. One study done recently in the United Kingdom showed that happy employees could be nearly 12 percent more productive, which is a rather significant amount. Not only that, but happy employees are also healthier, which means they take fewer sick days. It's hard to get work done when you're not feeling well. On top of that, the stock prices of the publicly traded companies on *Fortune*'s list of the top 100 companies to work for consistently outperform the rest of the market. You can't make your way onto this prestigious list without having truly happy employees.

# *Don't Be Afraid to...*
# Include Your Interests
# on Your Résumé

It's come to my attention recently that recruiters and résumé coaches are suggesting to their clients that they remove any mention of outside-of-work interests from their résumés and LinkedIn profiles. I've yet to hear a good reason for this. I can think of countless reasons why this is a terrible idea. But as long as recruiters and coaches are advising their clients to do this, the easier it will be for you to stand out from the crowd of professionals.

Several of the people I've interviewed have told me that they were hired specifically because of their outside-of-work passions. Mike Kelley is an accounting firm partner and an avid hockey and baseball player. This came up during his interview.

> I do talk with my senior partner, Otto Wheeler, quite a bit about baseball because he loves baseball, probably more than I do. It is one of the reasons I'm working here; in my interview, which was an unconventional interview to begin with because he doesn't care about all the political correctness of the interview process, he said, "All right, look, there are two men on, there's one out. It's a tie game.

What do you do?" I said, "You bunt." He goes, "You got the job." So my knowledge of baseball helped me get my job.

**MIKE KELLEY** HOCKEY/BASEBALL PLAYER

Just like all the other candidates, Mike was good at accounting. It was creating a connection with the managing partner that made a big difference for him. Had he not put that on his résumé or shared his interest during the interview process, he very well might not have gotten the position.

When I was looking to leave PwC, I had two lines at the bottom of my résumé:

- Professional stand-up comedian
- Big brother with Big Brothers Big Sisters of Central Indiana

And every single interview I went on involved talking almost the entire time about these two lines. Sure, we'd touch a little bit on my education and work experience, but the majority of the time was spent on the bottom of my résumé. Notably, each company I interviewed with gave me an offer.

Leaving these things off your résumé and LinkedIn profile is a sure way to *not* stand out and be noticed. Interests are a major way to differentiate yourself, so why wouldn't you include them?

# *Don't Be Afraid to...* Overcome Your Biggest Obstacle—Yourself!

As you've read this book, I'm sure there have been times when you've thought:

- "No one cares about my hobby."
- "My hobby has nothing to do with my job, so sharing is worthless."
- "People are going to think I'm not very dedicated to my company."
- "People are going to think I'm not good at my job."

All these thoughts are completely natural, and almost everyone I've interviewed has thought the same thing at some point in time.

Then they begin to share with someone in the office. That's when the magic happens. You'll realize that we aren't in seventh grade anymore and you aren't going to get ostracized for being unique.

Once others hear what you are passionate about, the right people are going to think it's amazing and want to know more. They're going to be genuinely interested, asking follow-up questions. They're going to hear the passion and excitement in your voice.

As is the case with so many professionals, the biggest critic will be you. No one is going to be as judgmental as you are of yourself, so start to share in a small way to gain some confidence and see that it really is just in your head.

> There was a time where I didn't talk about dance at work. I had this sort of dilemma, if you will, where I was trying to figure out how these things coexisted or did not coexist. For me, at one point, I actually separated them completely, meaning I had my business life and then I had my art life. That worked for a little while until I ended up in a hospital after having a panic attack. I never suffered from anxiety to that degree before. As I started to unpack that and gained some insights about who I was as an artist and who I was as a businessperson and how those things intersected, I realized that in the act of separation, I was creating a discordance with myself. That created the anxiety and the frustration and the challenges that I was having on multiple levels and I began to see how it was limiting my potential.
>
> **MATHEW HEGGEM** DANCER/CHOREOGRAPHER

# *Don't Be Afraid to...*
# Share Your "And"!

Your "And" is interesting, even to total strangers. I know this because when I'm flying and the person sitting next to me asks, "So, what do you do?" and I say that I'm a comedian and a speaker, we are talking all throughout the flight.

The conversation often starts with them saying, "Let me tell you who my favorite comedian is."

To which I say with a smile, "Let me guess, not John Garrett."

And then they proceed to go on and on about their favorite comedian.

If instead of saying I'm a comedian and a speaker, I tell them that I'm an accountant, they nod politely as they put on their noise-canceling headphones. We are done talking. No follow-up questions. Ever.

Imagine instead of a flight with strangers for a few hours, it's an office of coworkers that you see every day for eight hours or more. How miserable of a place would that be? No follow-up questions. No genuine interest in each other. No real emotion.

Unfortunately, that's what professionalism has encouraged us to create across the corporate world. The easiest thing you can do to break this mold is to share your "And."

# MODULE 3

# TAKING ACTION

By now you're probably thinking, "This sounds great in theory, but how do I put this into action? How do I go about implementing this at my organization?"

Every organization is unique. While some might be open to one idea, others will think it's the silliest thing they've ever heard. That's why when I consult with organizations on this, I always start by talking to the executive team so I can understand the parameters we can play with. The analogy I like is: Let's build the sandbox first and then let everyone play in it.

That's why I hesitate to tell you exactly how to do this at your firm or company. What I can do is provide you with some real-world examples that might be helpful to use as a starting point. Make them your own, build on them, and think of other ways to implement them in your unique way.

# Action Idea 1:
# Toastmasters Lunches

Many organizations like to offer skills development opportunities for their team members. One of the skills that most professionals could use some help with is public speaking, so why not offer them opportunities to do this in a low-stress situation? Some organizations have offered Toastmasters lunches once a month in the conference room. This ensures a smaller audience but also allows you to videoconference other offices that are doing the same thing.

The key is that the topic should always be "Your hobbies and passions outside of work." Bonus points if a speaker also adds how it makes them better at their job. This allows everyone to get public speaking experience in a safe environment, along with some coaching and feedback.

More importantly, because people are sharing their passions, they're growing closer together as they gain a better understanding of each other. HBK is a firm in Ohio, Pennsylvania, and Florida that has done this, leading to people in different offices developing stronger working relationships, often doing activities together on the weekends.

We're doing our own version of [Toastmasters] at lunch. We bring in some food and we have maybe two or three speakers and they talk for about five or seven minutes each. We have them talk about their hobbies and passions, because they can come in and talk about tax any day of the week. We want to see them stand in front of a podium and talk to an audience about something that they know without having to look at notes—and that, of course, is their hobby.

**JIM FAHEY**  CAR ENTHUSIAST

# Action Idea 2:
# Marketing Materials

To show what makes your organization different, remember the Culture Core model, which shows that you need to focus on your people's outside-of-work passions.

ACM is an audit and tax advisory firm in Colorado and Wyoming that has unique headshots on its website. Like most organizations, each member of their director/partner group has a separate biography page. What makes these biography pages unique is that each picture shows the person dressed in professional attire posed alongside something from their outside-of-work passion: mountain bikes, guitars, paintbrushes, board games, wrenches—and even a saddle.

Green Hasson Janks is an advisory firm that used a similar concept in its magazine ads and brochures to represent the firm's #BeMore philosophy, which featured photos of employees holding something from their passions under the slogan "That's How We Roll." The California-based firm's managing partner is holding a fishing rod, net, and tackle box, while others are shown with their pilot's headset, passport and suitcase, yoga mat, or chef's coat.

Yet another firm, Hawkins Ash, located in Wisconsin and Minnesota, created short videos of their employees participating in their hobbies. Each person is given a title, such as "Biker Dude," "The Explorer," or "The Happy Camper," before the firm's logo comes on the screen with the tagline "Driven by Passion." This sort of marketing can be used in a variety of ways, including on social media, embedded in your website, or even during live events.

All three of these approaches to marketing materials—digital, print, and video—allow people outside the organization to get to know its personality and what differentiates it from other service providers.

# Action Idea 3:
# Newsletters

This is something your marketing department or human resources department can handle. Most organizations have an internal newsletter sent to everyone on a regular basis. Add a section to the newsletter that showcases a different individual each week. In the piece, discuss the person's hobby or passion, include some pictures if possible, and then state how the person feels their hobby makes them better at their job. Then sit back and watch how this increases engagement.

# Action Idea 4:
# Nameplates and
# Business Cards

I recently saw the nametag of a pharmacist at a large grocery store chain. Right below her name, it said, "I'm interested in karate." And I immediately asked her about it. She's a black belt who started practicing karate later in life. It was clear she really enjoys it because her enthusiasm was infectious. And at no point did I think that she wasn't professional or wasn't good at her job.

Sure, most people who work in professional organizations don't wear nametags, but many organizations that have designated offices and cubicles have nameplates. How about adding some decoration or a Post-it Note attached below that says, "I'm interested in karate" or whatever that person's outside-of-work interest might be? Walking down the hall becomes fun as colleagues learn about a group of very interesting people who also happen to be good at their jobs.

# Action Idea 5:
# Email
# Signatures

I've seen this implemented and don't understand why it isn't the norm. Most organizations have a standard signature block at the end of a person's email that lists their name, title, etc. Adding space for their outside-of-work interests immediately after their work title allows everyone interacting with that person to create a deeper connection. Which, in turn, develops trust and leads to more enjoyable interactions—which makes work better.

Gusto, a payroll and human resources services company headquartered in San Francisco, does this. The last line of each employee's email signature is always their first name, followed by their hobby, and then the words "with Gusto."

> It's a really clever idea and I was curious to see what people did with gusto. My boss hunts for vintage treasure and I had another colleague who loves to dance to Bollywood music. It's always fun to see what people do. The signature block is a subtle way to let people know something about you. And yeah, you can ask them about it and they're always happy to talk about their interests.
>
> **CALEB NEWQUIST** BLOGGER

# Action Idea 6: Making Meetings Interesting

Let's face it, we've all sat in meetings completely zoned out, thinking, "This could've been an email." But for the meetings that are necessary, why not make them interesting? Why not make them fun and engaging? Why not give people a reason to pay attention so they actually hear what is said?

One way to increase engagement is for people to share a little bit about themselves.

At Pax8, they've had a rule from when they were founded that every new hire has to say something unique about themselves at their first monthly all-hands meeting. They have kept this tradition—and even expanded upon it—as they've continued to grow to over 400 employees.

> It really has carried over to any time we have an all-hands meeting or a larger meeting: Whoever stands up and speaks has to say something unique or interesting about themselves. And as a senior executive, you're speaking a lot, so you have to come up with a lot of things. But again, it's really encouraging everyone to get to know everybody a little bit and share a little bit.

As we continue to grow, the meetings become bigger and bigger. There was a discussion of "Should we just do the new-hire sharing quarterly?" And then we realized, "That's going to really be a big section where we introduce a lot of them," because we do not want that to stop. We need to keep going because it makes them memorable. More times than not, it's something you just always have in your head about that person. And it's just a lot of fun.

**J. KEITH** ARTIST

Another way you can encourage people to share is to extend your current meetings by three to five minutes. This works especially well with teams that meet regularly. Very similar to the Toastmasters lunches action idea, in each meeting have a different person do a short presentation on the topic of their outside-of-work hobby or passion. Not only does it give these individuals time to practice public speaking, it also allows everyone to get to know each other. Hearing the energy and enthusiasm someone has for their outside-of-work interest makes people more engaged, whether they have the same interests or not.

These simple ideas will result in stronger connections between your people. Sure, you're extending the meeting by three to five minutes, but you're also creating an engaging culture that encourages your teams to have a genuine interest in each other.

# Action Idea 7:
# Going to Lunch

Based on my own experience and what I've heard from clients, there can be some tension between departments. This is typically caused by the fact that interdepartmental relationships are based solely on work. If someone in one department makes a mistake, there is little forgiveness, patience, or understanding.

A simple way to address this issue is for someone in management to take two or three people from different departments to lunch—outside the office—and not talk about work. This helps bridge the gap by creating a real relationship that goes deeper than work. If you share similar interests, that's fantastic. But even if you don't, each person will gain a better understanding of the others and what they really enjoy doing. This translates back to the office the next time one of them needs to ask for something from the other side; they find they are now asking their new friend, rather than some random colleague. Both people now have a level of caring that usually makes them want to do better for each other.

# Action Idea 8:
# Recruiting

This is one of my favorite ideas and I've seen some clients use it very effectively. When a candidate visits for a round of interviews, companies often have someone act as their host. This internal person guides them around the office between interviews and might also take them to lunch.

Chances are good that you're very interested in this person if they've made it this far in the hiring process, so this is a fundamental moment for an organization to make a positive impression. Don't pick the host randomly. At the minimum, find someone who has something in common with the person coming in. Maybe it's where they grew up. Or maybe it's where they went to college. Or, better yet, maybe they share the same outside-of-work interest.

"But, John, how do we find that out?" You ask the candidate on the application. Or you ask them during your initial phone call.

You also need to create an internal document that lists each person at your organization and their corresponding outside-of-work interests. This is something that can be filled out by each person or you can designate someone to collect this information via email or by going around to talk with everyone. And because you've created a culture that shines a light on these activities, people will want to share at least one thing they enjoy doing.

By having the host be someone who shares a similar outside-of-work passion, you're showing the visitor that they already have a friend before they even start at the organization, which is huge. It also shows them that you've intentionally built a culture that values this side of people and you're not just talking about it. But most importantly, it shows them that they can be successful at your organization while also participating in their passions.

# Action Idea 9:
# Bucket Lists

I had the good fortune of visiting Teryn Grater in her office where I learned something cool that the firm does: It gives away bucket list experiences. Each person contributes two to three bucket list items to the office-wide list. At each quarterly all-staff meeting, one bucket list item is drawn from the list and the firm pays up to a certain limit for the winner to get that experience that they've always wanted to do.

For example, one employee always wanted to take high-end cooking classes, so the firm bought him a really nice set of knives and sent him to a chef school for a week. Another example is an employee whose husband is a firefighter, so the firm flew them both to New York City to go to the National September 11 Memorial & Museum and a show on Broadway. One employee wanted to ride in a hot air balloon, so the firm coordinated a trip for her and a few friends.

But this is the most critical part: After checking off the item from their bucket list, staff members share their experience, including stories, pictures, and videos, at the next all-staff meeting. And they talk about why it was a bucket list item for them. The powerful result is that people show real emotion in the workplace. Their peers are laughing and crying, drawn to each other like never before.

> We like to award people with some things that they just might not do otherwise. Sometimes just the smallest little nudge gives them a once-in-a-lifetime experience that they just wouldn't have done otherwise. And I think it does give us a closer tie to our people. Some of our employees have come back and told their stories and they have been real tearjerkers—the whole office crying in the training room. It's been really rewarding.
>
> **TERYN GRATER**  WORLD TRAVELER

# CONCLUSION

# Make Professionalism Weird!

I'm very fortunate that my speaking and consulting career allows me to travel all over the world. I did an event in Portland, Oregon, where the city has a saying borrowed from Austin, Texas: "Keep Portland Weird." Obviously, Austin's saying is "Keep Austin Weird." Although now that I think about it, that would be even weirder if Portland had kept "Austin" in there; it's surprising they didn't because Portland is ... weird. And they know it. Without a doubt, there are a lot of individuals there who are unique.

I want to borrow the idea from those cities, except we can't "keep" professionalism weird because, well, it's not. The working world is very stale and gray, full of people trying to conform to antiquated models of professionalism. Except we all now know that these stereotypes are completely wrong.

It's time we make professionalism weird!

My research has shown that there are so many unique individuals in the working world; we just haven't been encouraged to share what makes us different. You might be an accountant and a motorcycle racer. You might be an attorney and a musician. Or you might be an engineer and volunteer regularly. Share your "And" at work in the same way you share your technical expertise: only when needed and without hesitation. Our workplaces should allow us to outwardly express all aspects of our lives: university, continuing education, life experiences, and passions or interests outside of work.

Again, it's not *or*—it's *and*.

I didn't do well in physics class, but one of the things I learned is when two items collide, the one with the greater force makes a bigger impact on the other. For too long, professionalism has had the greater force and impacted you, making you feel like you needed to hide aspects of yourself. You've left a part of who you truly are outside the office every morning because you wanted to be "professional." Except each one of you *is* professional, so it's time you have the greater force and make an impact in your profession. I want you to make professionalism weird.

What do I mean by "weird"? I mean individual. Each one of you is the professional, so make your profession you. Make accounting you. Make law you. Make consulting you. Make engineering you. Make banking you. Because what you bring to your profession and what you bring to your job is different than the person sitting next to you. Totally different.

I can't do it alone, so I'm going to need you and all your friends and colleagues to help make this happen. Together, let's make professionalism weird!

**MAKE PROFESSIONALISM WEIRD!**

# Meet
# the Guests

It's been such a pleasure getting to know each of my podcast guests over the years. Here is a list, in alphabetical order, of the guests who were featured in this book. Now that their names have been in print, I fully expect them to rocket to the top of their respective organizations, soon becoming the CEO and/or managing partner. They're all cool people, so take some time to listen to their episodes and then look them up on LinkedIn. And if you're ever in their cities, tell them I said to reach out and say hello.

Ivy Anderson—consultant "And" photographer/ tae kwon do black belt—Chicago, IL (United States)

David Beasley—attorney "And" musician/composer— Las Cruces, NM (United States)

Rebecca Berneck—consultant "And" motorcycle racer—Chicago, IL (United States)

Dawn Brolin—accountant "And" softball player/ coach—Hartford, CT (United States)

Steve Browne—human resources "And" music lover—Cincinnati, OH (United States)

Donna Bruce—accountant "And" marathoner— Jackson, MS (United States)

Rumbi Bwerinofa-Petrozzello—accountant "And" film festival volunteer—New York, NY (United States)

Ashley Byma—accountant "And" cake decorator—Tucson, AZ (United States)

Jeff Crosley—marketer/software developer "And" pianist—Philadelphia, PA (United States)

Chris Ekimoff—accountant "And" swimmer—Washington, DC (United States)

Jim Fahey—learning officer "And" car enthusiast—Youngstown, OH (United States)

Rachel Fisch—accountant "And" singer/choir director—Toronto, ON (Canada)

Phil Gerbyshak—sales trainer "And" pinball wizard—Tampa, FL (United States)

Teryn Grater—accountant "And" world traveler—San Antonio, TX (United States)

Amy Hancock—engineer "And" model/photographer—Adelaide, SA (Australia)

Jason Hastie—accountant "And" country music singer/songwriter—Calgary, AB (Canada)

Mathew Heggem—consultant "And" dancer/choreographer—Alexandria, VA (United States)

Chris Hooper—accountant "And" weightlifter—
Adelaide, SA (Australia)

Hannah Horton—accountant "And" fiddler—
Louisville, KY (United States)

J. Keith—corporate development "And" artist—
Denver, CO (United States)

Mike Kelley—accountant "And" hockey/baseball
player—Austin, TX (United States)

Mark Lee—consultant "And" magician—London
(United Kingdom)

Andrew Logan—accountant "And" Harley-Davidson
rider—Saint John, NB (Canada)

Misty Megia—consultant/educator "And" theater
director/choreographer—Brentwood, CA (United
States)

Paul Meissner—accountant "And" curler—Melbourne,
VIC (Australia)

Ali Metzl—attorney "And" marathoner—Denver, CO
(United States)

Chris Morrison—accountant "And" adventure
photographer—Boise, ID (United States)

Brooke Mortensen—accountant "And" French horn
player—Helena, MT (United States)

Caleb Newquist—editor "And" blogger—Denver, CO (United States)

Tony Nitti—accountant "And" mountain biker/ backcountry skier—Aspen, CO (United States)

Clayton Oates—accounting technologist "And" world traveler—Alstonville, NSW (Australia)

Jody Padar—accounting technologist "And" reality TV fan—Chicago, IL (United States)

Abby Parsons—accountant "And" fiddler—Nashville, TN (United States)

Shannon Peters—attorney "And" guitarist—St. Louis, MO (United States)

MB Raimondi—consultant/trainer "And" stained glass artist—Knoxville, TN (United States)

Cindy Schroeder—bookkeeper "And" Disnerd— Orlando, FL (United States)

Daniel Siemens—accountant "And" ship in bottle builder—Denver, CO (United States)

Lauren Thiel—accountant "And" hip-hop dancer— Adelaide, SA (Australia)

Twyla Verhelst—accounting technologist "And" marathoner—Calgary, AB (Canada)

Ben Westbrook—operations "And" opera singer—
New York, NY (United States)

Mark Winburn—consultant "And" singer—Houston,
TX (United States)

# Acknowledgments

Writing a book is easily the most daunting thing I have ever done. I guess writing the acknowledgments means I'm finished! Getting to this point wouldn't have been possible without the encouragement and support of so many people along my journey. I'm honestly getting a little emotional thinking about it. If I truly thanked each of you, this book would easily be twice as many pages.

I'd like to thank everyone who has listened to me speak. Seeing your enthusiasm as you embraced my message propelled me to make writing this book a priority.

And thank you to each of my clients who have trusted me with their audience. I don't take that lightly. Your belief in my message made it even more rewarding to partner with you. It's been exciting to see how it has manifested itself at each of your organizations.

I'd like to thank the hundreds of you who have been on my podcast, sharing your hobbies and outside-of-work passions with the world. Your willingness to be vulnerable has encouraged so many others to do the same, helping create this movement. I'd also like to thank everyone who has listened to even just one episode because that's what keeps us recording new episodes every week.

And thank you to all my past coworkers. Little did I realize we were living this message from the beginning, so thank you for being a part of that.

To all the comedians with whom I've performed and to everyone who came to the comedy clubs where I've had the pleasure of taking the stage, thank you. Some of the comedians you've heard of, like Louie Anderson, Jimmy Brogan, Wayne Cotter, and Tom Wilson. And others you haven't, which is a shame because many of them make me laugh just as hard.

I'd like to thank Jesse Finkelstein and the team at Page Two for making this book so good. Your patience through this process allowed me to be confident in the final product.

It's important to say this book wouldn't have been possible without Chris Murray. You were my editor, my book coach, and, at times, my therapist. You understood my vision from the beginning and made writing a book an enjoyable experience. Every author should be so lucky to have someone like you by their side. I'm grateful to now consider you a friend.

A big thank you to Coach Holtz for believing in me enough to write the foreword to this book. You've had an impact on me personally since my freshman year at the University of Notre Dame, so this means more than I can say.

I'd like to thank those of you who personally held me accountable to finish this book. Your text messages, calls, and emails asking how the book was coming along were the gentle nudges I needed. I'd list your names but you know who you are because I have no doubt that you're reading this.

To my friends and family, I'd like to thank you for always being there for me. My career surely isn't conventional and it isn't easy explaining to others what it is I do for a living. And to my parents, I realize more and more the sacrifices you made so I could be where I am today.

And a special shout-out to my grandpa Rupert Macpherson, the first published author in the family. I miss you every day.

And finally, Brooke. Thank you for everything. I truly couldn't do any of this without you. Let's never stop dancing.

# References

## What Is Professionalism?

"Professionalism." *Merriam-Webster*, accessed June 5, 2020. merriam-webster.com/dictionary/professionalism.

McDowall, Duncan. *Quick to the Frontier: Canada's Royal Bank*. Toronto: McClelland & Stewart, 1993.

Diefenbach, Thomas, and Rune Todnem, eds. *Reinventing Hierarchy and Bureaucracy: From the Bureau to Network Organisations*. Bingley, UK: Emerald Publishing, 2012.

## Needed Now More Than Ever

"Talent Shortages at Record High: 45% of Employers Around the World Report Difficulty Filling Roles." ManpowerGroup, June 25, 2018. manpowergroup.com/media-center/news-releases/talent+shortages+at+record+high+45+of+employers+around+the+world+report+difficulty+filling+roles.

## Bring All of Yourself to Work

Aristotle. *The Nicomachean Ethics*. New York: Penguin Classics, 2004.

Grazer, Brian, and Charles Fishman. *A Curious Mind: The Secret to a Bigger Life*. New York: Simon & Schuster, 2015.

## Increasing Engagement

"The State of Employee Engagement in 2019: Leverage Leadership and Culture to Maximize Engagement." HR.com, May 2019. hr.com/en/resources/free_research_white_papers/hrcom-employee-engagement-may-2019-research_jwb9ckus.html.

McQueen, Nina. "Workplace Culture Trends: The Key to Hiring (and Keeping) Top Talent in 2018." LinkedIn, June 26, 2018.

blog.linkedin.com/2018/june/26/workplace-culture-trends-the-key-to-hiring-and-keeping-top-talent.

Malcolm, Hadley. "Millennials Will Take a Happier Workplace over Better Pay." *USA Today*, April 14, 2016. usatoday.com/story/money/personalfinance/2016/04/14/millennials-workplace-happy-salary-pay/82943186.

### The Cost of Turnover

Bersin, Josh. "Employee Retention Now a Big Issue: Why the Tide Has Turned." LinkedIn, August 16, 2013. linkedin.com/pulse/20130816200159-131079-employee-retention-now-a-big-issue-why-the-tide-has-turned.

### Broaden the Definition of "Expertise"

"Expertise." *Merriam-Webster*, accessed July 12, 2020. merriam-webster.com/dictionary/expertise.

"Expert." *Merriam-Webster*, accessed July 12, 2020. merriam-webster.com/dictionary/expert.

### Clients Will Trust You More

Kahneman, Daniel, and Amos Tversky. "Prospect Theory: An Analysis of Decision Under Risk." *Econometrica* 47, no. 2 (1979): 263–92. doi.org/10.2307/1914185.

Mann, Charles Riborg. *A Study of Engineering Education*. Pittsburgh, PA: Carnegie Foundation, 1918; quoted in Carnegie Foundation for the Advancement of Teaching, FAQs, September 8, 2014. carnegiefoundation.org/faqs/recently-read-somewhere-carnegie-foundation-report-said-85-persons-job-success-product-interpersonal-skills-15-success-result-technical-knowle.

## Technical Skills Don't Make a Leader

Haden, Jeff. "Here's How Google Knows in Less Than 5 Minutes If Someone Is a Great Leader." Inc.com, April 19, 2019. inc.com/jeff-haden/heres-how-google-knows-in-less-than-5-minutes-if-someone-is-a-great-leader.html.

## Reducing Anxiety and Depression

Linville, Patricia W. "Self-Complexity as a Cognitive Buffer Against Stress-Related Illness and Depression." *Journal of Personality and Social Psychology* 52, no. 4 (1987): 663–76. doi.org/10.1037//0022-3514.52.4.663.

## Make Better Ethical Decisions

Touré-Tillery, Maferima, and Alysson E. Light. "No Self to Spare: How the Cognitive Structure of the Self Influences Moral Behavior." *Organizational Behavior and Human Decision Processes* 147 (July 2018): 48–64. doi.org/10.1016/j.obhdp.2018.05.002.

Madhusoodanan, Jyoti. "Thinking of Your Work Self as Separate from Your Home Self Could Lead to Unethical Decisions." *Quartz*, October 31, 2018. qz.com/work/1436230/thinking-of-your-work-self-as-separate-from-your-home-self-could-lead-to-unethical-decisions.

## We Need Human Connection

Maslow, Abraham H. "A Theory of Human Motivation." *Psychological Review* 50, no. 4 (1943): 370–96. doi.org/10.1037/h0054346.

Rutledge, Pamela B. "Social Networks: What Maslow Misses."
*Psychology Today*, November 8, 2011. psychologytoday.
com/us/blog/positively-media/201111/social-networks-
what-maslow-misses-0.

Tay, Louis, and Ed Diener. "Needs and Subjective Well-Being
Around the World." *Journal of Personality and Social
Psychology* 101, no. 2 (June 2011): 354–65. doi.org/10.1037/
a0023779.

Rath, Tom. *Vital Friends: The People You Can't Afford to Live
Without*. Washington, DC: Gallup Press, 2006.

Murthy, Vivek H. *Together: The Healing Power of Human
Connection in a Sometimes Lonely World*. New York: Harper
Wave, 2020.

Rath, Tom, and Jim Harter. "Your Friends and Your Social Well-
Being." Gallup News, August 19, 2010. news.gallup.com/
businessjournal/127043/friends-social-wellbeing.aspx.

## Become a Friend, Not a Colleague

Mirza, M. Aslam. *Project Management and Leadership
Challenges, Volume II: Understanding Human Factors and
Workplace Environment*. New York: Business Expert Press,
2018.

## Increase Trust and Oxytocin

Halford, Scott G. *Activate Your Brain: How Understanding Your
Brain Can Improve Your Work—and Your Life*. Austin, TX:
Greenleaf Book Group Press, 2015.

Uvnäs-Moberg, Kerstin, Linda Handlin, and Maria Petersson.
"Self-Soothing Behaviors with Particular Reference to
Oxytocin Release Induced by Non-noxious Sensory

Stimulation." *Frontiers in Psychology* 5, no. 1529, January 12,
2015. doi.org/10.3389/fpsyg.2014.01529.

## Best Versus Different

Godin, Seth. *Purple Cow: Transform Your Business by Being
Remarkable*. New York: Portfolio, 2003.

## *Don't Be Afraid* ... Even If This May Not Be Easy

McCabe, Sean. "Why Hobbies Matter in and out of the Office."
*Accounting Today*, April 3, 2017. accountingtoday.com/news/
why-hobbies-matter-in-and-out-of-the-office.

## *Don't Be Afraid to* ... Let People Do Their Extracurricular Activities

Revensecio, Jonha. "Why Happy Employees Are 12% More
Productive." *Fast Company*, July 22, 2015. fastcompany.com/
3048751/happy-employees-are-12-more-productive-at-work.
Strahlberg, David. "The Best Places to Work: Delivering Strong
Results Compared to the S&P 500 over 10 Years." *Seeking
Alpha*, June 18, 2019. seekingalpha.com/article/4270853-
best-places-to-work-delivering-strong-results-compared-
to-s-and-p-500-over-10-years.
Yoshimoto, Catherine, and Ed Frauenheim. "The Best
Companies to Work for Are Beating the Market." *Fortune*,
February 27, 2018. fortune.com/2018/02/27/the-best-
companies-to-work-for-are-beating-the-market.

# About the Author

John Garrett—thought provoker, catalyst for change, and podcast host—is on a mission to create better workplaces. What the two-time Emmy nominee may do best is champion the human side of professionals, consulting with organizations to develop more productive cultures while  shining a light on their people's rich lives outside of work. Delivering inspiring keynotes about his research and recording over 300 podcast episodes of *What's Your "And"?* landed him on *Accounting Today*'s list of the top 100 most influential people in the profession.

John received his bachelor's degree from the University of Notre Dame, where he earned a letterman jacket as a trombone player in the marching band. He went on to pass the CPA exam and received his certified public accountant certificate while working at PwC and performing stand-up comedy as a hobby.

Since then, he's been on stage over 2,000 times and tracks from his debut album, *Outside the Box*, can be heard on several channels on SiriusXM Satellite Radio and Pandora. He's also been on *The Bob & Tom Show*, featured in the *New York Times*, opened for Louie Anderson at resort casinos, opened for the band Train, and has been invited to perform at several comedy festivals.

John currently lives in Denver with his wife and enjoys watching college football and eating cookie dough ice cream—especially at the same time.

For more information about John and the services he offers, visit TheJohnGarrett.com.

# Let's Keep in Touch

**I feel like our journey together is just beginning.**

So here we are at the very end of the book! Since you've made it this far, you're either lost or this message resonated with you. I wrote *What's Your "And"?* with the belief that it would positively influence the way people interact with those around them.

If you would like to keep the momentum going, share your copy of the book with someone who will appreciate the message. And while you're busy sharing, how about taking a minute to leave a quick review on Amazon? Amazon reviews seem to be the most common way books are judged and your review will help future readers appreciate what they're in for.

If you've got a large group of people who would benefit from a copy of this book, the least I can do is coordinate a bulk order to help you save money. Are you looking to make a more significant impact? My team is able to create custom versions of the book, complete with colors to match your brand. Please email speaking@ thejohngarrett.com if you'd like your audience to remember who introduced them to this movement.

## Let's hang out

Visit WhatsYourAnd.com for links to follow me on social media, watch my music video parodies, subscribe to my podcast, or send me a message. I would love to hear the different ways your organization is encouraging people to share their "And." Be sure to use #WhatsYourAnd so I'll see your pictures and posts.

## Be on my podcast

Let's tell your story. We'll talk about your "And" and how sharing it has impacted your career.

## Use *What's Your "And"?* for your book club

Get your friends and coworkers talking about how to implement this philosophy at work. Email bookclub@ thejohngarrett.com for the complimentary Book Club Discussion Guide.

## Bring me in for speaking and consulting engagements

One of my favorite things to do is engage with audiences to help them learn to use their full skill set by sharing their outside-of-work passions. And what I find most rewarding is helping companies implement ideas to enhance their Culture Core to retain top talent and build lasting relationships with clients.

Let's chat about the impact you'd like to make and how I can help.

**WhatsYourAnd.com**